# Designing Interactive Multimedia Systems

To Jamileh, Anoosheh and Mitra
the bright lights of my life

# Designing Interactive Multimedia Systems

M. Dastbaz

THE McGRAW-HILL COMPANIES

**London** · Burr Ridge IL · New York · St Louis · San Francisco · Auckland
Bogotá · Caracas · Lisbon · Madrid · Mexico · Milan
Montreal · New Delhi · Panama · Paris · San Juan · São Paulo
Singapore · Sydney · Tokyo · Toronto

**Designing Interactive Multimedia Systems**
M. Dastbaz
ISBN: 007709863 3

Published by McGraw-Hill Education

**Mc Graw Hill**

Shoppenhangers Road
Maidenhead
Berkshire
SL6 2QL
Telephone: 44 (0) 1628 502 500
Fax: 44 (0) 1628 770 224
Website: www.mcgraw-hill.co.uk

**British Library Cataloguing in Publication Data**
A catalogue record for this book is available from the British Library

**Library of Congress Cataloging in Publication Data**
The Library of Congress data for this book has been applied for from the
Library of Congress

Acquisitions Editor:        Conor Graham
Editorial Assistant:        Paul Von Kesmark
Senior Marketing Manager:   Jacqueline Harbor
Senior Production Manager:  Max Elvey
New Media Developer:        Douglas Greenwood

Produced for McGraw-Hill by Steven Gardiner Ltd
Text design by Steven Gardiner Ltd
Cover design by Design Deluxe
Printed and bound in Great Britain by Bell and Bain Ltd, Glasgow

# Contents

# Preface

Looking back at the beginning of the 1990s, it is remarkable to see how computer technology has developed and how it has fundamentally changed almost every aspect of our lives. As the managing director of a computer company called Systems 2000 Ltd in 1990, we were assembling Intel's 80386 machines with 16 MHz of processing speed, 1 MB of Ram and 40 MB hard disk. At the time these eight-bit slow beasts were state of the art desktop machines running mostly under DOS (Disk Operating System) aimed at bringing 'real computing power' to businesses and individuals. Compare that with the present desktop PCs, an integrated environment capable of handling information in a rich variety of formats including audio, video and text and as well as reaching 2000 MHz of speed, with possibility of 1 GB of Random Access Memory (RAM) and tens of GB of hard disk storage and one could clearly see Moore's law in action.[1]

Although there were significant advances in the 1970s and 1980s in terms of developing desktop machines, it was in the 1990s when the desktop PC revolution started in earnest. As a result personal computers emerged as a mass-market commodity triggering massive investments by large IT corporations resulting in a boom in the development of new innovative hardware and software tools.

So what do we mean by Interactive Multimedia Systems. The book will

---

[1] Gordon Moore was one of the eight founders of the Fairchild Semiconductor Company, which went on to establish Intel. Moore in his famous 1965 article titled: 'Cramming more components onto integrated circuits', contemplating the future shape of the IT revolution predicted that the number of transistors per integrated circuit would double every 18 months.

provide you with detailed discussion about the concept, the history and present status of the multimedia technology. At this point it is sufficient to state that multimedia is referred to as the integration of audio, video, animation, graphic, and text in an interactive environment controlled by a desktop PC. Therefore, when we refer to Interactive Multimedia Systems it is not a simple combination of various types of medium but rather a new integrated environment that is capable of processing information in a variety of formats not possible before. Hence the term Interactive Multimedia Systems.

Looking back at the literature, published in the early 1990s, it is not hard to detect that the emergence of the Multimedia technology was greeted with scepticism especially amongst academic circles. Multimedia technology was dismissed as nothing but a gimmick by the computer industry seeking new areas of growth. Indeed I can recall an article by Ian Ritchie, who later on become the president of the British Computer Society, in the October 1992 issue of CTISS files, where he slammed the hype surrounding the emergence of multimedia stating that: 'In reality their offerings are neither unique, nor available yet in economically deliverable format, nor in many cases remotely suitable for the purpose they proclaim'.

The view regarding the importance of multimedia is very different today. We have been learning and exploring the technology during the last decade and multimedia has become one of the key components in a convergent technological drive. Massive investments have been made developing the multimedia technology particularly mobile multimedia, i.e. delivering multimedia content to mobile devices and the pressure on academic institutions to deliver courses relevant to the shortages of key skills needed has resulted in enormous growth of courses in multimedia technology. The fact that UK universities alone offer more than 500 courses and units on multimedia or related topics and hundreds of courses are offered in the USA and European countries is testimony to the growing need for relevant textbooks and learning resources needed in delivering these courses.

Teaching various units on Interactive Multimedia Systems (IMS), over the last five years, I have always found it difficult to suggest an appropriate single textbook that deals sufficiently with the design, development and evaluation aspects of interactive multimedia systems. The idea for this book was therefore, to produce a stand-alone text that provides the readers with sufficient in-depth knowledge about theories and concepts behind what we call interactive multimedia systems as well as providing practical guidance, in the shape of case studies, on how one would go about designing and implementing such systems.

Furthermore, the emergence of the Internet, as a global network of millions of computers, and the emergence of the World Wide Web, as the means of exchanging information within this network has created a media rich global information super-highway that requires particular attention. While with the first generation of interactive multimedia systems we were mainly concerned with CD-ROM based delivery platform with the emergence of the WWW, interactive multimedia is rapidly becoming an on-line environment with its specific challenges in design and development.

## THE STRUCTURE OF THE BOOK

The book is divided into five sections and twelve chapters, taking the reader from introductory level topics to advanced design and development stages of interactive multimedia systems.

The first section of the book introduces the reader to the history of emergence of multimedia as well as other key concepts such as Hypertext and Hypermedia. Section two of the book provides a discussion on multimedia hardware, software and tools. The third section looks at the design development, and evaluation of interactive multimedia systems. Section four of the book discusses multimedia on-line and introduces issues involved in delivering multimedia content on the WWW. Finally the last section of the book is aimed at providing a glimpse into the future by means of an introductory discussion on mobile multimedia computing.

## KEY FEATURES

Each chapter of the book contains a brief summary of key points discussed. Further-more, each section of the book includes a number of questions and projects intended to help the reader focus on the topics discussed. The projects are designed as open-ended challenges requiring further research and considerable analytical and in some cases practical work. These projects have no simple or single answer. There could be different approaches and methods to tackle them achieving varied and valid solutions. The projects could also be attempted as a collaborative exercise where readers could work together to find the solutions. Each section also includes suggestions for further reading, which consists of useful books or academic journals that could be helpful to the readers who require a more in-depth probing of the topic discussed. It is also worth mentioning that all the citations used throughout the book along with the suggested reading are included in the bibliography provided at the end of the book.

## ACKNOWLEDGEMENT

I am indebted to many people for their help during the last year. I would like to thank Alfred Waller who got me started on this project, when he was at McGraw Hill. I would also like to thank Conor Graham, his editorial team at McGraw Hill, and Steven Gardiner for their help. I am grateful to the reviewers, who read the initial proposal and saw the final product. Their comments and criticism helped me enormously in putting the final touches to the book. I would also like to thank many of my colleagues who took the trouble of reading the manuscript for their helpful comments as well as constant support and encouragement. These include: Prof. Kalafatis, at Kingston Business School, who encouraged me to start my research on Multimedia systems, in 1992; Prof. Hashim, head of School of Computing at South bank University who has been a tremendous support over the last two years; other colleagues at South Bank University who gave me encouragement including; Michael Macaulay, Ebad Bannisi, Anna Pollard, Robin Whittey, and Geoff Elliot. I would also like to thank Lesley Ledden, at Kingston Business School, for helping me with many IMIS projects, over the past five years, and for allowing me to use her video clips in the book. Thank you to Annik Hogg who believed in me and supported me when I first started doing research on Multimedia and finally to my family who put up with me for the past year and helped me complete this project.

# Part I

# Interactive Multimedia Systems

## History, Definition, Key Concepts and Application Areas

*This section presents a brief historical overview of the development of the IT technology in general and the emergence of Interactive Multimedia Systems (IMS) in particular. Key related concepts such as hypertext and hypermedia as well as application areas for IMS are also discussed.*

# 1

# A Historical overview

*'Here we are at the threshold of a new age of interactive text graphic and audio and of course, here I am still writing about it in a linear fashion! Let us enjoy the moment and strike while the irony is hot...for it is time to celebrate what is to come, little though we know what that my be.' (Nelson, 1989)*

## 1.1 THE CONCEPT

More than half a century ago, Vannevar Bush, director of the 'Office of Scientific Research and Development' and an advisor to the US president, Roosevelt, described a hypothetical machine that would allow users to browse through a media rich environment making associative links between various types of information. He envisaged a device called 'memex' in which an:

> *'Individual stores his books, records and communications and which is mechanised so that it may be consulted with exceeding speed and flexibility. It is an enlarged intimate supplement to his memory.'*

(Bush, 1945)

This simple and yet interesting and innovative proposition forms the fundamental theoretical background upon which present-day interactive multimedia systems are based. The question that immediately comes to mind is why has it taken more than half a century for Bush's idea to be realised? In order to find a satisfactory answer to our question the reader must note that fifty years ago the computer technology was in its infancy. Therefore it follows that the history of the development of Interactive Multimedia Systems is directly and closely linked to the history of the development of the personal computers.

## 1.2 THE HISTORY: FROM PUNCH CARDS, TO MULTIMEDIA PCs

The history books linked the idea of computers to the first attempt in building mechanical calculators. Blaise Pascal presented one such idea in 1643. He proposed

**Fig. 1.1**  A view of ENIAC

and built *Pascaline*, the first mechanical calculator. Later, in 1822, Charles Babbage developed the *Analytical Engine* that used *punch* cards to tell the machines what numbers to calculate. It was in the 1940s (about the same time that Bush was proposing the *memex* machine) that significant advances were being made in the development of computers. Mauchly and Eckert built the first 'digital' computer at the University of Pennsylvania in 1946. It was called the ENIAC (Electronic Numerical Integrator and Calculator).

ENIAC could perform 5000 arithmetic calculations per second. However, the physical dimensions of ENIAC meant that it could not be used outside the laboratories where it was built. ENIAC weighed 30 tons, stood two stories high and covered 15,000 square feet of floor space. It contained some 19,000 vacuum tubes, 70,000 resistors, and 10,000 capacitors. ENIAC was a major breakthrough but nevertheless it was not a practical tool by any means, as it required 200,000 watts of power to operate.

Consequently, the early generations of computers were not widely available. It was in the 1970s, following the launch of Intel's new chip called the 8000 series of microprocessors and the Apple computer that the significant changes began to take shape.

## 1.3    THE EMERGENCE OF THE MULTIMEDIA PC (MPC)

The rapid development of the microprocessor industry in the 1980s and 1990s resulted firstly in the emergence of powerful personal computers, and secondly in the availability of the technology to the large proportion of the population. Further

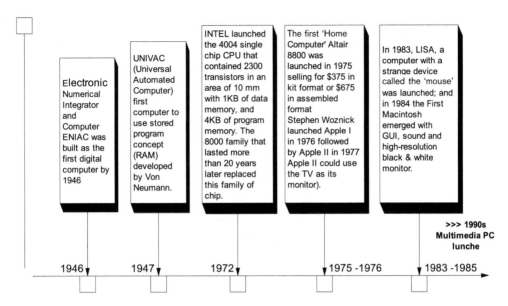

**Fig. 1.2**   Time-line of important developments leading to the emergence of Multimedia PC

developments in the manufacturing industry in the 1990s, particularly the emergence of Compact Disk (CD), audio and video technology, paved the way for Multimedia extensions to the PC and hence the birth of the Multimedia PC. In 1991, leading hardware and software companies in the personal computer industry discussed the future development of the PC market and agreed that the way forward was to integrate various existing mediums, such as sound, and live video into one. As a result, two industrial groups were formed. One consisted of 85 firms led by the Microsoft Corporation and was called the Multimedia PC (MPC) Marketing council. The other group consisted of 200 companies, led by IBM and Apple, and was called the Interactive Multimedia Association (IMA). Both groups announced their intention to develop and release MM PCs towards the end of 1992 and the beginning of 1993. The MPC group was the first to announce a set of definitions and standards for a MM PC, reviewed for a brief period of time (MPC-I, MPC-II and MPC-III) and then abandoned as a result of rapid technological changes.

The reader should also note that also crucial to the rapid development of IMS was the parallel and rapid growth of graphical user interfaces and operating systems. Perhaps the most important of all these developments was the launch of Microsoft's **Windows**™ operating system that paved the way for a move from 'text based' operating systems (i.e. CP/M, DOS, etc.) to an **Apple**™ like graphical user interface with built-in support for multimedia extensions such as sound and video.

| Hardware | MPC I | MPC II | MPC III |
|---|---|---|---|
| CPU | 386sx (16 Mhz) | 486sx (25 Mhz) | Pentium (75 Mhz) |
| Random Access Memory (RAM) | 4 MB | 8 MB | 16 MB |
| HD drive | 30 MB | 160 MB | 500 MB |
| Audio Card | 8 bit + MIDI | 16 bit + MIDI | 16 bit + MIDI |
| Video Card Resolution Colour Depth | VGA 640 ×480 256 (8 bit) | SVGA 640 ×480 65K (16 bit) | SVGA + MPEG I 640 ×480 65K (16 bit) |
| CD-ROM speed seek time Storage Capacity | Yes 150 Kb/s 600 ms ~ 650 MB | Yes 300 Kb/s 400 ms ~ 650 MB | Yes 600 Kb/s 280 ms ~ 650 MB |

### Current typical Multimedia PC Specifications:

- **CPU**: Pentium IV or equivalent Microprocessor 2 ~ 2.5 GHz
- **RAM**: 128 MB ~ 1 GB
- **Hard disk Capacity:** 10 GB ~ 100 GB
- **Audio Card**: 64 bit Stereo with Midi
- **Video Card** - 32 MB video Ram 1024 ×768
- **Video Capture card**: allowing video capture and playback
- **CD-ROM**: write and re-write technology with
- **Digital Video Disk:** (DVD) drive (30 hours of analogue video storage)
- **Built-in Modem:** for connecting to the WWW

**Fig. 1.3**   Multimedia PC standards

A more detailed treatment of multimedia hardware and software is provided in Section two of the book.

The developments mentioned above signalled the emergence of the Multimedia PC but the reader needs to distinguish between a multimedia PC and an interactive multimedia system. While a multimedia PC is nothing but a desktop PC with audio, and video capabilities, an interactive multimedia system, as suggested by Bush, is an integrated environment which is capable of processing information in a variety of media rich formats not possible before.

## Chapter Summary

- The concept of Interactive Multimedia Systems originated from Vanvar Bush's memory extender (Memex) idea presented in his paper titled 'As We May Think' in 1945.
- It was not until the 1970's with the emergence of more powerful computers that possibilities for implementing his ideas became a reality.
- Multimedia PC can be defined as a desktop personal computer with audio, video, graphic, text and animation capabilities.
- Also crucial to the rapid development of multimedia systems was the parallel and rapid growth of graphical user interfaces and operating systems.
- While a multimedia PC is nothing but a desktop PC with audio, and video capabilities, an interactive multimedia system, as suggested by Bush, is an integrated environment which is capable of processing information in a variety of media rich formats not possible before.

## Exercises and Projects

### PROJECT

This is a group project aimed at carrying out extensive research on Multimedia technology and its various application areas. The research should cover some or all of the following areas:

- History and background on the emergence of Multimedia
- Hardware & Software development of Multimedia systems
- Emergence of Hypertext & Hypermedia
- Emergence of Internet and the WWW
- Application areas for Multimedia Systems

### RECALL QUESTIONS

1. When was the first digital computer built and what was it called?
2. What key developments in the manufacturing industry in the 1990s resulted in the emergence of the Multimedia systems?
3. What do MPC and IMP stand for?
4. What key development in operating system development was also crucial to the development of Interactive Multimedia Systems?

# 2

# Application areas for Interactive Multimedia Systems

*'Wholly new forms of encyclopaedias will appear, ready-made with a mesh of associative trails running through them... All our steps in creating or absorbing material of the record proceeds through one of the senses – the tactile when we touch keys, the oral when we speak or listen, the visual when we read. Is it not possible that some day the path may be established more directly?' (Bush, V. 1945)*

With the emergence of Multimedia technology in the early 1990s it was also recognised that apart from the need to expand and accelerate the work in overcoming the early technical problems it was also important to clarify and clearly communicate the applications and benefits of MM technology. The purpose of this chapter is not to serve as a comprehensive enumeration of all the wide and varied range of applications of interactive multimedia systems rather as a brief overview of what is possible and what has been achieved thus far.

## 2.1    EDUCATION

Education undoubtedly has been one of the main beneficiaries of the emerging multimedia technology. For decades the progress of Computer Aided Learning CAL packages within the education system was hampered by a number of issues such as presentation of subjects in the face of limitations imposed by the 'text-based' systems. Areas such as a hard-to-reach event like a theatrical performance, a therapy session, a volcano in eruption, or a group interview or the visual effectiveness of a particular advertisement were all out of reach for CAL packages. CAL packages

**Fig. 2.1**   Screen capture from the business research methods developed by the author as a learning aid for MBA students

at best could communicate a description of the events listed in a similar fashion to written text.

The emergence of multimedia and the integration of video, sound and animation offered the all-encompassing medium, which enabled CAL designers to create a much richer learning environment. The technical advancements also allowed designers to design for greater levels of interactivity within CAL systems. Hutchings (1992) noted that multimedia enhanced CAL encompasses the modes of learning and interaction associated with conventional CAL, but it allows greater learner control, access to MM learning materials and a variety of modalities of interaction with the learning material, which are only now becoming apparent.

The 1990s witnessed an explosion of CD-ROM based learning materials. Everything from multimedia encyclopaedias to a wide variety of CD-ROM based learning aides as well as multimedia enhanced distance learning packages were developed and a number of research studies indicated that multimedia based learning could be used effectively as a mode of delivery.

Furthermore, the European Commission set up the 'Industry Research Task Force on Educational Software and Multimedia', which began its work in March 1995. In its first report in July 1996, the 'Task Force' stated that: '*Stimulated by the steady fall in multimedia equipment prices, the mass market for educational multimedia – both products recorded on optical disks (CD-ROM and CD-I) and services which can be accessed by the telematic networks – can not fail to grow rapidly in the mid 90s'.*

According to this report the design, development and evaluation of educational MM is one of the key areas of research development within the European Community, which requires urgent attention. Multimedia based learning has been further effected by the emergence of the World Wide Web and the emergence of Web-based multimedia learning termed generically as Electronic Learning (E-Learning). Many educational institutions now offer courses through the Web and with the rapid development of the Web technology overcoming the initial communication limitations including the availability of broadband and fibre optic technologies the path of growth and further development of on-line interactive multimedia learning environments is very clear.

The 'global' nature of the technology driven education also raises some very important questions. Borders and countries no longer bind the competition between education institutions. The WWW provides a global 'virtual campus' that students from all over the world could attend. Education could be delivered where and when is demanded. This clear shift in teaching and learning paradigms, from time and placed bound instruction to free, exploratory and self paced constructive approach has also raised fundamental issues about the future of the education system in its present structure. There are those, who predict that as a result of the emerging technologies universities in their current format would not survive. Peter Drucker, in an interview with the *Forbes Magazine* (1997) stated:

> 'Thirty years from now, the big university campuses will be relics. Universities won't survive... Do you realise that the cost of education has risen as fast as the cost of health care?... Such totally uncontrollable expenditure without any visible improvement in either the content of the quality of education, means that the system is rapidly becoming untenable. Higher education is in deep crises... Already we are beginning to deliver more lectures and classes off-campus via satellite or two-way video at a fraction of cost. The college won't survive as a residential institution...'

## 2.2   TRAINING

A study by the US Department of Defence found that MM training was roughly 40% more effective than traditional training, with a retention rate that was 30% greater and a learning curve that was 30% shorter (Shulman, 1992). This is further supported by a number of other studies, which have shown that interactive training increases retention, decreases cost and reduces the amount of time required in training sessions. Increasing flexibility in work schedules and location of work will demand more flexible means of delivering training courses and will require the provision of just-in-time distributed learning that is tailored to individual needs (Israel, 1992). The literature further points that MM should be viewed as an enabling tool, which could help executives to manage staff training and education. Many large corporations use their network structures particularly their Interanets (Internal Internets) to design and

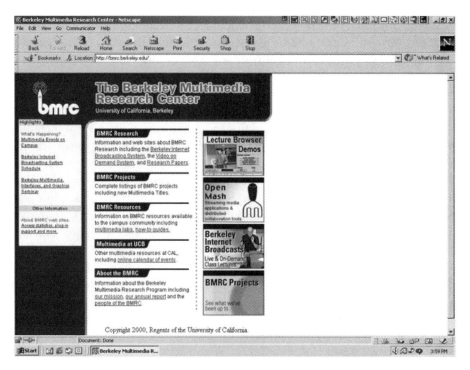

**Fig. 2.2**  A Berkeley University Internet Broadcasting System offering full course on-line (http://www.bmrc.berkeley.edu/).

develop self-paced training packages for their staff (a generic term used for such an approach is Electronic Training or E-Training). Amongst the advantages of E-training one could point to the convenience it offers staff to go through the material at their convenience and a suitable pace. Furthermore, multimedia enhanced training packages could use video, audio and animation to create a richer learning environment. Training on the use of sophisticated equipment could be simulated and users could easily master the use of such equipment inside computer-simulated environment.

## 2.3   POINT OF SALES INFORMATION

An early example of MM in sales can be found in Spears (1987) who describes the work of Lawrence Marshall Production (Toronto, Ontario) and in particular a project to promote real estate in Canada. In a variety of centres (including airports, the New York's World Financial Centre etc.) MM kiosks, equipped with hardware devices that permit integration of video, graphics and audio with

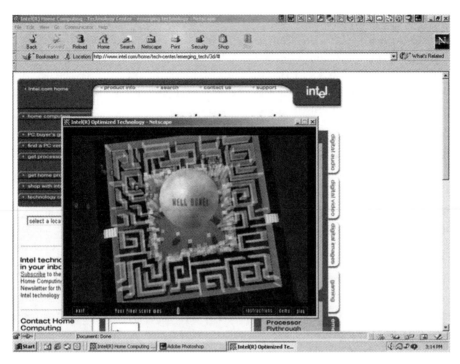

**Fig. 2.3**   Intel Corporation uses Multimedia to train its staff on sophisticated chip manufacturing machinery (http://www.intel.com/)

**Fig. 2.4**   A Multimedia kiosk

touch-screen input devices, are used to direct visitors around the large complexes. Some state authorities in USA have employed the provision of information about government services, through interactive touch-screen MM systems. A good example of use of Multimedia kiosks in Britain could be seen at the natural science museum where multimedia information kiosks provide visitors with valuable insights to the exhibits around the museum.

## 2.4    NEWS DELIVERY, BROADCASTING AND ADVERTISING

Broadcasting and advertising has been one of the main beneficiaries of interactive multimedia systems. As early as 1992 Liebman recognised that there is increasing demand for broadcasting and advertising agencies to move towards the use of interactive media. Intelligent electronic catalogues, disk-based advertising, desktop presentation systems and the MM advertising approach are among the areas that have benefited from the emergence of multimedia.

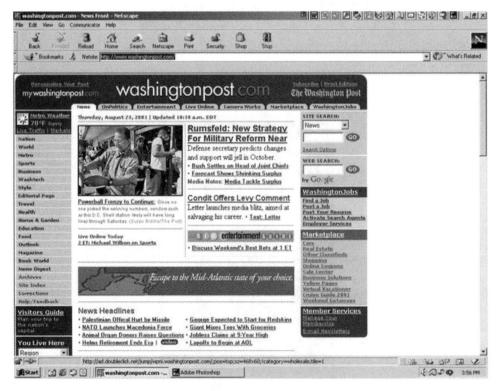

**Fig. 2.5**  The Washington Post web site with many added features as compared to the printed version (http://www.washingtonpost.com/)

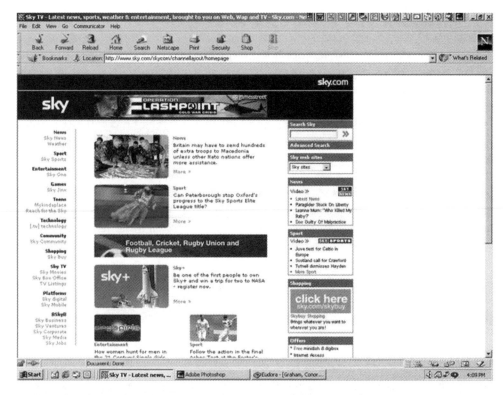

**Fig. 2.6**   Sky Corporations TV Channels on the Web (http://www1.sky.com/skycomHome/home-page/)

The launch of interactive TV and the ever-increasing capability of the WWW (including Web TV and Web casting) to present media rich information have added new interesting and exciting dimensions to traditional approaches. Even traditional means of delivering news like newspapers have undergone major changes trying to embrace the new technology.

Browsing through the Web one could find thousands of newspapers in tens of different languages bringing up-to-date news to millions of Web surfers. The inter-active nature of the Web also allows for news providers to enrich their traditional mainly text-based content by adding live reports and video clips as well as offering their customers sophisticated search facilities and 'push' technology to send users specific news on demand.

Even traditional news broadcasting corporations like the BBC and CNN are allocating enormous budgets in developing Web-based news delivery and Internet channel that offers 24 hours day, seven days a week news to users when and where they required it.

## 2.5   COMMERCE AND BUSINESS APPLICATIONS

Despite a very sluggish start for developing real applications for interactive multi-media systems, the emergence of the Web, a global market of tremendous market value, have quickly changed the initial dismissive attitudes towards the effectiveness of the technology and what it could offer today's businesses. Even the most conservative sections of the business world, the banking industry, have embraced the technology and are seeing the new technology as new channels of distribution capable of reaching new markets with enormous potentials.

The primary impact of the Multimedia technology, particularly the WWW, on business and marketing is to break the time and location bound aspects of traditional commerce (Sheth & Sisodia, 1999). Customers, be it individuals or companies, can place orders, gather information and communicate with each other from any place at any time. Companies large and small are able to achieve high level of accessibility and

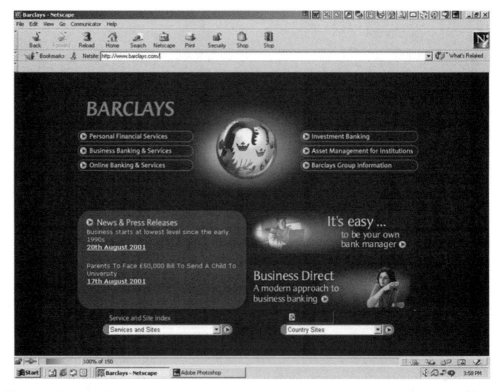

**Fig. 2.7**   Barclays Bank on-Line services offering full on-line banking and share dealing (http://www.barclays.com/)

establish a two-way information flow directly with end users almost immediately and at a low cost. Based on such a model every company is global player from the first day of its existence. Among some of the success stories about marketing and commerce on the net, one could mention Amazon.com, (world's first on-line bookstore, which recently announced a 230% increase in its net sales from $87.4 million to $293.6 million in its first quarter. The company now boasts a customer base of over 8 million people all over the world and is segmenting its market into CD's, Video and on-line auctions) and the giant US computer firm Dell which is selling millions of PC's through Internet channels.

The technology is shifting business and marketing paradigms. The old model of the 'one-to-many' process whereby a firm communicates its message through a medium to a large group of consumers is being replaced by a model in which a many-to-many process exists, with greater control and freedom of choice passed on to consumers.

Academics and business leaders alike argue that the Internet simply has not been around long enough for a distinctive body of knowledge and theory to develop. This may be so but the pace of change and emerging technologies, such as digital television and moves towards more convergence between various technologies are such that they demand immediate attention from academics and practitioners alike. In the words of Michelangelo: Ancora imparo – 'I am still learning', but we have to be quick learners to keep pace with exciting and important developments that awaits us in the 21st century.

## Chapter Summary

- Multimedia technology have a wide range of application areas including:
  - Education: e.g. hypermedia/multimedia aided learning, e-learning... etc.
  - Training: e.g. Web-based training
  - Point of sales and information: e.g. multimedia kiosks
  - News delivery, broadcasting and advertising: e.g. Web TV
  - Commerce and business: e.g. e-Commerce and m-Commerce.
- The technology is shifting business and marketing paradigms and the old model of the 'one-to-many' business process is being replaced by a 'many-to-many' model.

# Exercises and Projects

## PROJECT

- Write a report about the effect of multimedia technology in the delivery of news around the world. Your report should carry out a comparative study into the traditional method of news delivery (i.e. printed papers, radio and TV) and compare it with the current ways of delivering news. The report should cover areas such as:
    - Web TV
    - Web radio
    - Use of streaming technology, etc.

## RECALL QUESTIONS

1. How can multimedia enhance the delivery of learning in 'hard to reach' events like a theatrical performance?
2. Name different application areas for multimedia kiosks.
3. Discuss the difference between 'push' and 'pull' technology as far as delivery of information on the Web is concerned.
4. What are the key effects of the emerging multimedia technology on small and large companies in terms of accessibility and information flow.

# 3

# Multimedia, Hypertext and Hypermedia Relationship and Links

*'... so quick bright things come to confusion.' (A Midsummer Night's Dream)*

Sifting through the early literature and even some more recent papers and articles one could not help noticing that the terms multimedia, hypertext and hypermedia have sometimes been used loosely and inter changeably, thus creating a certain amount of confusion as to the relationship and links between these very distinctly separate but perhaps related concepts. In Chapter one we discussed the concepts and ideas behind multimedia and more importantly what we mean by interactive multimedia systems. The aim of this chapter is introduce the readers to the concept of hypertext and hypermedia and then link the three together.

## 3.1  HYPERTEXT AS A CONCEPT

Hypertext emerged as a concept in the 1940s and later refined in the 1960s. Ted Nelson first coined the term hypertext in his well-known article 'The Literary Machines' in 1965 and it is only during the last two decades that attempts have been made to implement hypertext using emerging technologies. It is therefore important to distinguish between hypertext as a concept for organisation of ideas and information and hypertext as a set of technologies (e.g. The World Wide Web – WWW).

Landow (1997) wrote that the problem of causality is that it is not always possible to determine what has caused a specific change in a science. According to him the concept of hypertext is one that has emerged as a result of the convergence between theorists, concern with literature and theorists, concern with computing.

Bush in 1945 presented the scientific community with a pioneering view about information filled environment that is modelled on human brain with its associative nature and accessibility. He predicted:

> *'Wholly new forms of encyclopaedias will appear, ready-made with a mesh of associative trails running through them... The owner of the memex, let us say is interested in the origin and properties of the bow and arrow. Specifically he is studying why the short Turkish bow was superior to the English long bow... He has dozens of possibly pertinent books and article in his memex. First he runs through an encyclopaedia, finds an interesting but sketchy article, leaves it projected, next, in a history he finds another pertinent item, and ties the two together...'*

The above idea as expressed by Bush (1945) forms the corner stone upon which the concept of hypertext is built. Furthermore, according to Landow (1997) contemporary theorists both in literature and computing, e.g. Jacques Derrida, Roland Barthes, Theodor Nelson and Andreas van Dam, have been arguing that the hypertext concept is based on abandoning the conceptual systems found on ideas of centre, margin, hierarchy, and linearity and replacing them with ones of multi-linearity, nodes, links and networks. He also points out that this paradigm shift can be viewed as a direct response to the strength and weaknesses of printed book (discussed later in this chapter).

What distinguishes hypertext from written and printed text is the associative structure of hypertext, which closely models the structure of human memory. This concept was clearly outlined by Bush (1945) who stated that the human mind operates by association. With one item in its grasp, it moves in accordance with some intricate web of trials instantly to the next that is suggested by the association of thoughts.

Hence, the concept of hypertext could be described by its two main characteristics.

Firstly as a tool that would 'mimic' the human mind in terms of links and associations.

Secondly as a new way of presenting and accessing textual information (and in the case of hypermedia other types of information such as sound, video and animation). The latter also aims to overcome a number of problems associated with written and printed text such as:

- Sequential access: text-based information is arranged in a rigid sequence.
- Lack of associative learning and information gathering: For example a book or a document does not allow its reader to gain in-depth information about a specific topic which is not the main subject area of the book or the document.

- Lack of efficient retrieval mechanism: text-based information does not provide the user with the mechanism to search its content in an efficient and flexible manner in as many different ways as the reader requires.

It is in the early 70s that systems developers became interested in these ideas and started looking at different ways that the concept of hypertext could be implemented as a set of technologies. Andries Van Dam (1987), started his keynote speech to the 'Hypertext '87' conference by asking why it had taken so long for the idea to become reality.

> *'Why did it take so long to have this workshop, to have HyperCard, when the technology certainly has been out there and there have been a lot of proof of concept demonstrations? Well the first reason is the classical inertia problem. Why did it take twenty years for Doug Englbart's mouse to be commercialised?...New ideas take forever to be popularised. The second reason is of course that there are technology problems...'*

## 3.2   EARLY HYPERTEXT TECHNOLOGY AND IMPLEMENTATIONS

The first attempt to implement the concept put forward by Bush and Nelson was made in 1968. Doug Englbart conducted a live demonstration of his 'Augment system' at the Joint Computer Conference in which he worked collaboratively on a hypertext document with a colleague 500 miles away (during the same session he also demonstrated the mouse for the first time). Conklin (1987) in his survey of the hypertext history describes some of the most important early attempts at hypertext implementation, including the following systems:

- **Augment/NLS**, NLS was the first (oN Line System) that had hypertext like features.
- **ZOG**, a high performance hypertext system used aboard the USS Carl Vinson. ZOG was the predecessor of KMS (Knowledge Management System which was designed to manage fairly large hypertext networks across local area networks).
- **Intermedia**, developed by a research group at Brown University. Intermedia was an integrated environment that allows different types of applications (word processors, editors and other programs) to be linked together.
- **NoteCard**, developed at Xerox was a hypertext system for designers, authors and researchers to analyse information, construct models, formulate arguments and process ideas.
- **Xanadu**, a concept of 'docuverse' (document universe) developed by Ted Nelson where everything should be available to everyone and any user could follow origins and links of material across boundaries of documents, servers, networks and individual implementation (see Figure 3.1).

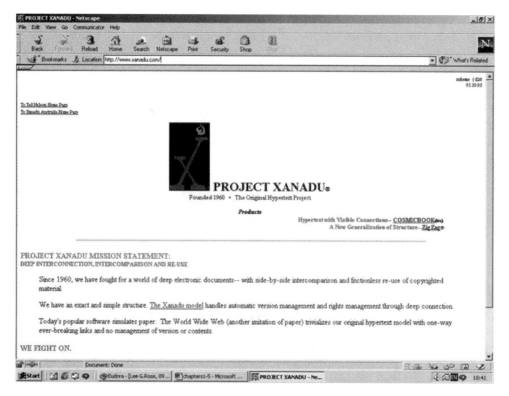

**Fig. 3.1**   Screen shot from Project Xanadu's Web space (http://www.xanadu.com/)

The early attempts at implementing hypertext clearly proved that hypertext can be a very powerful tool which can offer information system developers enormous possibilities. The early hypertext developers recognised that the technology was still in its infancy and as Van Dam (1987) concluded in his closing remarks at 'Hypertext '87' the road ahead was long and bright.

> 'We are just at the beginning and it's too early to rush to judgement, but it's clear that collectively we have a lot of hard work to do to make this technology work and create what has been called the electronic Alexandria.'

## 3.3   DEFINING HYPERTEXT

The literature on hypertext offers a wide variety of definitions (see among others Nelson, 1967; Conklin, 1987; Smith, 1988; Beagoray, 1990; Brown, 1991; Nielsen, 1991; Carr, 1994; Halasz, 1994; Bloomfield, 1994; Nielsen, 1995; Kendall, 1996; Kolb, 1997). Ted Nelson (1967) described a hypertext system as:

*'a combination of natural language text with the computer's capacity for interactive branching, or dynamic display... of a non-linear text... which can not be printed conveniently on a conventional page.'*

Conklin (1987) noted that the concept of hypertext is quite simple. It consists of windows on the screen that are associated with objects in a database and links are provided between these objects. Begoray (1990) stated that a defining characteristic of hypertext is a network representation of information through a link structure.

It is believed that the variety of definitions offered for hypertext is due to the absence of a clear theoretical basis behind hypertext and the fact that hypertext remains a largely technology driven field (Bloomfield, 1994). On the other hand the literature reflects a more unified set of definitions of the components within a hypertext system, i.e. nodes and links.

Hypertext literature also offers differing models to describe the relationship between links and nodes. A typical hypertext systems is shown in Figure 3.2.

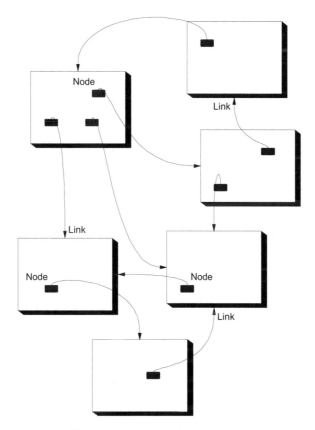

**Fig. 3.2**  A typical Hypertext system

The following discussion on the key components of hypertext is offered in order to present an overall explanation of hypertext systems.

### 3.3.1  Hypertext Elements

#### (i)  Nodes

Nodes store the system's complete information and display it to the user and can contain a variety of information such as text and graphics. Conklin (1987) stated that although the essence of a hypertext is its machine-supported linking, the nodes contribute significantly to defining the operation that a hypertext system can perform.

With the development of computer systems over the last four decades, important changes have taken place in the way that nodes are designed and implemented in hypertext systems. Early hypertext systems such as NLS and ZOG allowed only text to be stored in nodes. Later systems such as HyperTies, HyperCard and Guide allowed bitmap pictures and charts to be stored and displayed. Current hypermedia systems allow for a richer variety of information, including text, bitmaps, audio, video and animation to be stored as nodes.

In addition to context the issue of node size has also been subject to significant changes. Carr (1994) noted that early hypertext systems only allowed for rigidly fixed sized nodes (i.e. amount of information stored in a node). This restriction particularly affected the design and implementation process of early systems. Fixed node sizes force the system's author to either edit or cut the amount of information to fit in within the node, or to split the node into two or more nodes. In conclusion nodes provide the vehicle for the representation of ideas, facts and concepts in hypertext systems Conklin (1987).

#### (ii)  Hierarchies

Some hypertext models allow for nodes to be organised in hierarchical structures. Although this hypertext feature is not widely cited in the literature, the existence of hierarchical structures within some hypertext model is, nevertheless, important. Such structures improve navigation and reduce disorientation within hypertext. The hierarchical structure forces authors of hypertext systems to sort the nodes into a number of sets and introduce categorisation (i.e. grouping nodes together based on their types). The hierarchical structure of hypertext systems also allows for the main node ('parent') to be linked to several nodes down the hierarchical tree ('child') nodes. Mohageg (1992), commenting on the hierarchies within hypertext systems, pointed out that hierarchical structures are suited for hypertext systems or text intensive database systems which are used for retrieval of the information.

### (iii)   Anchors

Conklin (1987) noted that hypertext systems require a mechanism for addressing or referring to locations or items within the content of an individual component. This mechanism is known as 'anchoring'. Halasz and Schwartz (1994) pointed out that anchoring allows hypertext structures to create links not only between documents but between objects within one document and objects within another document.

### (iv)   Links

Links in hypertext systems are defined as the means of connecting nodes. Links are perhaps the most fundamental notion of hypertext systems. The main function of links is to provide a logical navigational mechanism in a hypertext document. Garzotto *et al.* (1995) summarised the role of links as 'representational' and 'navigational'. The representational role is to capture and represent relationships and the navigational role is to show paths down which the user may navigate. Researchers (see among others: Conklin, 1987; Garzotto *et al.*, 1993; Carr, 1994; Bloomfield, 1994) have identified a number of different types of link that could exist within a hypertext system. Conklin (1987) refers to the following three distinguishable types of link:

- **'Referential links'** are used for explicitly linking two points (nodes) in a hypertext system. They generally have two ends, a start and an end point and are usually directional, i.e. forward or backward links.
- **'Organisational links'** are similar to 'referential links' in that they connect two explicit nodes within a hypertext system. 'Organisational links' differ from 'referential links' in that they are used to implement a hierarchical structure, i.e. connecting a 'parent' node with its 'children'. DeRose (1989) refers to these links as 'Inclusive' links and describes them as links that allow the connection of one location to many target locations and represent super/subordinate (i.e. parent/child) relationships.
- **'Keyword links'** – Conklin (1987) commented that, as well as explicit linking performed by referential and organisational links, there is also the 'keyword link' structure that occurs through the use of keywords.

The above discussion on hypertext is offered as a guideline on how a hypertext system could be recognised. As stated at the beginning of this chapter, the literature offers a diverse range of views and definitions on hypertext. The discussion of hypertext and its components was presented in order to facilitate the debate on hypertext design issues (design models, link structures, etc.) that follows.

## 3.4   HYPERMEDIA

The term hypertext implied a system that deals only with text. With the integration of sound and video technology into the desktop PC and the emergence of MM systems, the term hypermedia has been used for hypertext systems that are capable of linking together more than just textual information.

Bevilacqua (1989) compares hypermedia to the invention of alphabetical order or Plato's dialectical argument as principle of organising knowledge which combines text and non-text data such as graphics or digitised sound. Carroll (1993) states that the term hypermedia is used now to refer to computer information systems that provide access to multimedia databases (i.e. to databases incorporating graphics, image, sound, video and text). The above have been synthesised by Akscyn *et al.* (1994) who describes a hypermedia system as a generalisation of a hypertext system which could be characterised by the following features:

- Information, be it text, sound, live video, animation or drawing, is presented in 'chunks'.
- Information displayed in units per one window (i.e. separate objects).
- Units of information inter connected via links.

Consequently, hypermedia can be viewed as the next development stage of hypertext. Although all basic principles and characteristics associated with hypertext apply to hypermedia systems, the additional technological extensions to hypertext (i.e. sound video etc. see Figure 3.3) bring with them advantages as well as problems and complications for the design of such systems.

## 3.5   MODELLING HYPERTEXT AND HYPERMEDIA

### An Overview of Data, Process and Design Models

It was not until the late 1980s, following 'Hypertext '87', that attempts were made to propose a general purpose design model for hypertext systems. This was mainly due to the lack of appropriate hardware and software development to allow large scale implementation of such systems. It was in the late 1980s, with the emergence of desktop computers and powerful programming tools, that development in the design and implementation of hypertext/ hypermedia systems occurred. Since 'Hypertext '87', a number of researchers (see among others Campbell and Goodman, 1988; Stotts and Furuta, 1989; Hardman *et al.*, 1993; Gronbaek and Trigg, 1994) have proposed various models for hypertext/hypermedia design.

A number of these models (i.e. HAM, DHM, CMIF to be presented later in this chapter) have been developed as a result of attempts to implement hypertext systems in a specific context and therefore their usefulness in defining a general purpose design model is limited. Another problem associated with some of the models (i.e. HAM, Tower presented later in this chapter) is that they tend to deal with low-level system issues such as 'host file system' rather than deal with top-level design issues such as user interface. Nevertheless the author feels that the reader would

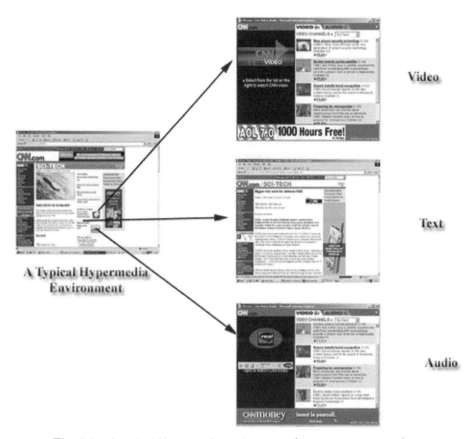

**Fig. 3.3** A typical Hypermedia environment (http://www.cnn.com)

benefit from gaining some understanding of the important research work carried out in early stages of the development of hypertext and hypermedia with direct consequences to the work that currently is being undertaken to further develop hypertext and hypermedia both as a concept and as a set of technologies.

## 3.6 HYPERTEXT ABSTRACT MACHINE (HAM)

Campbell and Goodman (1988) presented a key paper at the 'Hypertext '87' conference which could be viewed as the first attempt to define a reference model, i.e. an abstract model in which hypertext systems could be expressed. They called their model the 'Hypertext Abstract Machine' (Figure 3.4) and defined it as follows:

> 'The Hypertext Abstract Machine (HAM) is a general purpose, transaction-based, multi-user server for hypertext storage system... The HAM stores all of the information

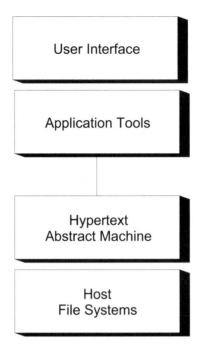

**Fig. 3.4** Hypertext Abstract Machine (adapted from Campbell and Goodman, 1988)

*it manages in graphs, or databases, on a host machine's file systems... The HAM storage model is based on five objects: graphs, context, nodes, links and attributes.'*

As can be seen from the above figure, HAM does not describe a complete hypertext system and is positioned between the file system and the user interface. Campbell and Goodman (1988) pointed out that HAM is designed as a general-purpose hypertext engine and could be used as a base engine for the design of other hypertext systems. However, it is difficult to substantiate this claim since HAM's main emphasis is almost solely on the storage model of a hypertext system (i.e. the file host system) with little attention paid to the application and user interface layers. Campbell and Goodman (1988) concede that although HAM is not a panacea for hypertext data storage problems, it is an important first step. HAM's contribution is to offer a formal definition of hypertext systems and their relationship with their environment.

Looking at Hypertext architecture, the WWW follows closely the three level architecture discussed in HAM. The lowest level is the 'data base level', which consists of Internet and all the computers connected together globally. All these computers (servers) provide their data to the clients (users) in a standardized format called HTML (Hypertext Markup Language) through a standard communication protocol called HTTP (Hypertext Transfer Protocol). The combination of HTML and HTTP forms the Hypertext Abstract Machine (HAM). The users could use a variety of software running on a variety of computers as long as they talk HTTP and understand HTML. The presentation level of the model is handled by the client viewer running on user's machine (for more details see Nielsen, 1995) A more detailed discussion of the Internet and the WWW is presented in Section 4).

## 3.7   DEXTER'S HYPERTEXT REFERENCE MODEL

In October 1988 at the Dexter Inn in Sunapee, New Hampshire, a workshop organised by John Legget and Jan Walker brought together a group of hypertext designers. The work of this so-called 'Dexter group' resulted into a data and process model that acted as a reference standard and paved the way for the emergence of more comprehensive data and process models.

Hardman *et al.* (1993) stated that the Dexter model introduced the concepts of components (both atomic, i.e. singular 'objects' and composite, i.e. components that are formed from several atomic 'objects'), links and anchors. Components (called nodes in system implementations) are related to each other via links and the anchors specify the location of the ends of the links. The Dexter hypertext reference model (Figure 3.5) separates a hypertext system into three different layers called the 'run-time layer', the 'storage layer' and the 'within-component layer'.

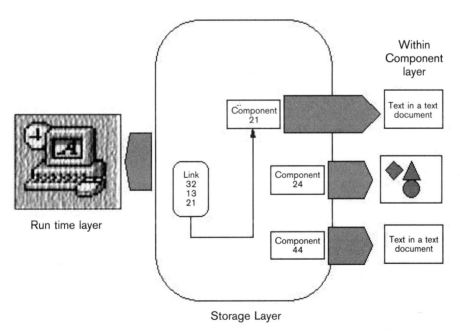

**Fig. 3.5**   Layers of the Dexter model (adapted from Gronbaek and Trigg, 1994)

1.    **The run-time layer:** The run-time layer deals with the issues regarding how the hypertext system is presented to its users. Halasz and Schwartz (1994) stated that hypertext provides tools for the users to access view and manipulate the network structure. The run-time layer of the model captures this functionality, according to them. They further note that the range of possible tools for accessing, viewing and manipulating hypertext is far too diverse to allow a simple and generic model. Hence the Dexter model provides only a skeleton model of the mechanism for presenting a hypertext to users.

2.    **Storage Layer:** The main focus of Dexter's model is on the storage layer that defines the basic node/link structure. The storage layer effectively describes a 'database' that is composed of a hierarchy of data containing 'components'. The components in this layer are treated as generic containers of data and no attempt is made to model any structure within the container. Thus the storage layer does not differentiate between text components and graphic components.

3.    **The within-component layer:** This layer is mainly concerned with the contents and structures *within* the components of a hypertext network. According to Halasz and Schwartz (1994), this layer is not elaborated within the Dexter model. The range of possible contents/structures that can be included in a component is therefore not restricted. Text, graphics, animation, simulations, images and other types of data could be used as components. They further note that the Dexter model treats the within component layer as being outside the hypertext model and assumes that other reference models designed specifically to model the structure of particular applications, documents or data types will be used in conjunction with the Dexter model.

The Dexter model is the first data and process model that defines a clearly layered and modular structure for hypertext systems. The author agrees with Gronbaek and Trigg (1994) who points out:

> 'Though the Dexter model is not intended for system developers, a measure of its success is that it has nonetheless served as a starting point for the design of hyper-media systems'.

Some of the shortcomings of this model have been addressed by subsequent design models, which are described later in this chapter.

## 3.8    THE TRELLIS HYPERTEXT REFERENCE MODEL (R-MODEL)

Stotts and Furuta (1989) proposed a hypertext design model called the '*Trellis hypertext reference model*' abbreviated as *r-model*. The r-model divides a hypertext system into the following five levels:

- **Abstract component level:** This level presents the components that will be associated with one another in order to form the hypertext. This layer describes the system *structure* (the Trellis system uses a network structure), *abstract contents* (that could include textual, graphical, animated, audio or video type of material), *abstract buttons* (abstractions of the relationship among the content elements), and *abstract containers* (an abstraction of how the pieces of hypertext will be combined when shown to the reader).
- **Abstract hypertext level:** The elements of the abstract component level need to be connected together to form the hypertext system. This connection or association is defined in the abstract hypertext level.
- **Concrete context level:** This level describes the mapping from hypertext abstract representation to its physical representation (e.g. how are buttons to be displayed? Are the buttons triggered 'static' or created as a result of other events or computational processes 'dynamic'?).
- **Concrete hypertext level:** This level maps the concrete representations into a set of windows for display. The concrete windows representation also determines the link-based relationship between the windows (i.e. the process of following a link could result in several different display mappings).
- **Visible hypertext level:** At this level, the details of the concrete hypertext to be transformed to visible presentation for the readers/ users are specified.

The r-model is essentially designed to be used for large distributed environments such as computer networks. Although the r-model is a clear attempt to clarify and further modularise hypertext systems, like the Dexter model, it does not deal with specifics, particularly the area of user interface. The r-model is also primarily a hypertext design model, rather than a hypermedia design model and does not attempt to deal with time-based issues such as integration of video, sound and animation and their impact on the design of such systems.

## 3.9   THE TOWER HYPERTEXT MODEL

DeBra *et al.* (1992) presented an object oriented data model for hypertext at the fourth ACM hypertext conference (1992) which has come to be known as the 'Tower Model' and is illustrated in Figure 3.6.

The model, while containing all the basic structures and elements of a typical hypertext system, such as nodes and links, also includes what the authors call *tower objects* (composite nodes see Figure 3.6) and *city objects*. The *tower* objects are used to model different descriptions of an object while *city* objects represent a view of the object. Another feature of this model is that it allows all objects to be virtual objects (i.e. the results of a function or an algorithm).

DeBra *et al.* (1992) explain in their paper that their model is made of two layers. The lowest layer defines primitive objects like nodes, links and anchors. While

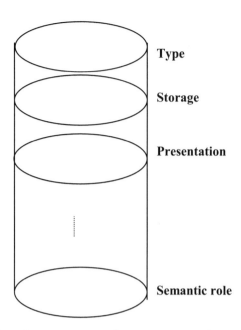

**Fig. 3.6** 'Tower' for a text node (adapted from DeBra *et al.*, 1992)

the second layer consists of modelling constructors which build complex information representations out of the simpler ones. They go on to point out that their model could also be regarded as an interface layer that, once supported by different information sources, would permit their integration within the hypertext system. The authors also state that while other design models like Dexter, HAM etc. aim at standardising hypertext design, their model is aimed at forming the basis for implementation of such systems.

The primary concern of this model is the data structure aspect of hypertext systems. The model tends to view hypertext as a tool for integration of different information sources and lacks specific design guidelines, such as link structures and directionality. On the positive side, the tower model, attempts to address some of the shortcomings associated with the Dexter's model, namely the with-in component layer and data structures in hypertext systems. The contribution of the r-model lies in its attempt to offer a detailed definition of hypertext's data structure.

## 3.10   CMIF MULTIMEDIA MODEL

Developed by the '*Centrum voor Wiskunde en Informatica*' (CWI: Centre for Mathematics and Computer Science in Amsterdam), the CWI Multimedia Interchange

Format (CMIF) describes a model for representing and manipulating multimedia documents. Presented by Hardman *et al.* (1993), the CMIF introduces the time-based organisation of information. According to Hardman *et al.* (1993) media objects in CIMF have contents that could be played as well as synchronisation constraints that are used to specify timing information among the objects. The resulting document can be played as if it was a video sequence, with the user/reader having control over playing, stopping or pausing the presentation. Hardman *et al.* (1993) states that CMIF system includes the following components:

- **Data block:** This contains data of an atomic medium (similar to Dexter's atomic component).
- **Channel:** This is an abstract output device for playing events, i.e. a window on the screen or audio output.
- **Synchronisation arcs:** These are used to specify timing constraints between data blocks.
- **Data descriptors:** These are a set of attributes describing the structure of a data block.
- **Event descriptor:** These are a set of attributes that describe the presentation of one instance of the data block.

The fact that CMIF allows for the composition of static and dynamic data into a time-dependent presentation is an important step forward in addressing issues omitted from the models discussed so far in this chapter. The major drawback with the CMIF model is that it does not include links, instead it represents presentation order and conceptually is viewed as a multimedia presentation model rather than hypertext/hypermedia model.

## 3.11 AMSTERDAM HYPERMEDIA MODEL (AHM)

In order to overcome the shortcomings listed above, the CWI presented the Amsterdam Hypermedia Model (AHM) which enables the description of structured multimedia documents. Like CMIF it incorporates time as well as extending the notion of links to time-based media and composition of different media. Hardman *et al.* (1993) noted that the Dexter model was created to describe hypertext and the CMIF was developed as a model for multimedia presentation. Whilst both models have their advantages and drawbacks there was a need to develop a design model for hypermedia systems.

The AHM extends the Dexter's and the CMIF in the following areas:

- **Composition with multiple, dynamic media:** Allows the grouping of items into a presentation and the expression of timing constraints between these items. Also defines hypermedia links that take readers/users to destinations consisting of a variety of items of static and dynamic media grouped together to form a presentation.

- **Higher level presentation:** Allows for predefined sets of presentation specifications which can be applicable to a number of objects, i.e. similar to style templates defined in sophisticated word processing packages.
- **Combining composite components:** Allows for combination of various dynamic media to create a complex presentation.
- **Temporal relations:** Recognises and allows time-based relations that are treated as presentation information.
- **Context for links:** Allows for link context information specifying whether, when following a link the reader/user will end up with a new presentation or a part of the current presentation being replaced.

AHM is essentially based on Dexter and the CMIF models and represents an important step in trying to overcome the drawbacks and shortcomings associated with both these models. The AHM emphasises the importance of composition, and utilises this for building structured documents. It also allows for temporal (time-based) relationships as well as introducing link context.

Therefore AHM could be viewed as the first attempt to introduce a model for a hypermedia system combining the Dexter's hypertext model and the CMIF multimedia presentation model. However, just like the Dexter model the AHM deals with general aspects of developing a hypermedia system.

## 3.12   DEVISE HYPERMEDIA MODEL (DHM)

Proposed by Gronbaek and Trigg (1994), this model is, once more, based on Dexter's model and results from an attempt to implement an open hypermedia system. The model includes an object-oriented database and extends the concepts of links within the Dexter model. Gronbaek and Trigg (1994) pointed out that in their implementation of links they confronted two problems with Dexter's model: firstly the way it deals with 'dangling links' (i.e. links without a clear start or end point), and secondly the notion of link directionality (i.e. forward, backward, etc.).

According to Gronbaek and Trigg (1994), the Dexter model includes limited provisions for link directionality such as: FROM, TO, BI-DIRECT, or NONE depending on whether the end point is to be interpreted as a source, destination, or neither. Gronbaek and Trigg (1994) discussed the following three notions of directionality that could extend Dexter's model:

- **Semantic direction:** This concerns the semantic relationship between the components represented by the link.

- **Creation direction:** This direction indicates the order in which the link end points were created, the source of the link being the first end and the destination being the last.
- **Traversal direction:** This direction specifies how the link can be traversed. For example, in HyperCard, links can only traverse from source to destination, while in NoteCard, links can be traversed in both directions.

The other area that the DHM extends the Dexter model is the way anchors are defined. The Dexter model identifies anchors as a means of referring to the 'within components'. The DHM distinguishes the following three high-level anchor types that are independent of the type of the enclosing component:

- **Marked anchors:** Where an object is directly embedded in the component's contents, i.e. visible icons inserted in text or graphic windows. This is called a link marker.
- **Whole-component anchors:** That deals with link end points not anchored within the component's contents.
- **Unmarked anchors:** These are anchors that have no link markers. For example DHM supports a kind of unmarked anchor called *Keyword anchor* within the text components.

It is clear from the above that the DHM attempts to extend and further clarify particular issues such as link directionality and types of anchors within the Dexter model that are important for the development of Dexter based hypermedia systems. Like other models reviewed so far, DHM is mainly concerned with low-level structural design of hypertext systems and does not address higher level design issues such as user interface as well as temporal issues (such as video and animation) that have emerged with the integration of other media into hypertext.

## 3.13   THE HYPERMEDIA DESIGN MODEL (HDM)

The Hypermedia Design Model (HDM) was developed as part of the HYTEA project by an European Consortium led by Garzotto *et al.* (1995) and has since been widely used by more than twenty development groups in six different countries. Garzotto *et al.* (1995) describe the following four concepts as the building blocks of the HDM model:

- **In-the-large:** The overall hypermedia application organisation and behaviour.
- **In-the-small:** The details of the application's organisation and behaviour.
- **Structure (in-the-large, in-the-small):** The way in which the content of the application is organised.
- **Dynamics (in-the-large, in-the-small):** The description and the way the application behaves.

HDM model divides the hypermedia systems into the following components and parts:

- **Slot (in-the-small):** This is an atomic (primitive) piece of information that could be as simple as an integer or as complex as a video clip synchronised with sound. Multimedia slots could have very complex structures such as control sets for video playback.
- **Frame (in-the-small):** This is an aggregate (sum) of slots that together form a granule of information. In HDM, a frame is a presentation unit that is shown to the user.
- **Nodes (in-the-small):** The HDM model views a node as a navigational unit and each node is usually associated with a unique frame. In HDM, nodes of the same type have similar frames and connections.
- **Components (in-the-small):** These are formed from a group of nodes to create a logical unit. For example a component called 'Paint' could consist of a bitmap, sound, and a text part.
- **Collection (in-the-large):** This refers to a set of objects. A collection member could include, components, single nodes and other nested collections. For example in a hypermedia package Art Gallery (by Microsoft) a collection could include all the paintings on a given subject.
- **Links (in-the-large):** HDM defines links as a connection between two different objects. Links provide the mechanism for moving from the sources to the destination as well as presenting and, in some cases, activating the destination. The destination is always a node. The HDM also allows for time-dependent media and the state in which to leave the source (i.e. reset to original state or leave as modified by activation). HDM allows for a number of different types of links, including structural links (a connection between two different objects, i.e. nodes), collection links (that link together the collection-node and collection members according to their logical structure) and index links (that connect the collection nodes to each member of the collection). Figure 3.7 gives an overview of the HDM's link structure as implemented with the 'Piero della Francesco' hypermedia system (Garzotto *et al.* 1995).

As can be seen from Figure 3.7, the 'Piero della Francesco' hypermedia system has a top-down link structure where users traverse from a root component (PFn) down to lower layer nodes (p1-n). However, the root structure as presented in the above figure is not very well defined in terms of return pathways and links for users. Following the AHM (Amsterdam Hypermedia Model) the HDM is a step forward in developing a design model for hypermedia systems. HDM overcomes a number of important shortcomings associated with the HAM and the Dexter models, particularly in dealing with time-based multimedia elements within a hypermedia system and the increasingly complex nature of the links within such systems. A drawback with the HDM model is the way link structures are proposed. Although the proposed parallel organisation of links offers a number of possibilities in linking a 'parent' node to its 'children', it

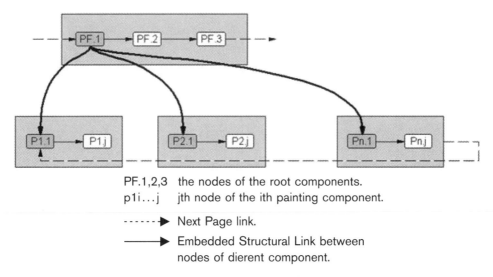

PF.1,2,3   the nodes of the root components.
p1i...j    jth node of the ith painting component.

------▶  Next Page link.

————▶  Embedded Structural Link between
         nodes of dierent component.

**Fig. 3.7**   A view of an HDM Hypermedia system (adapted from Garzotto *et al.*, 1995)

nevertheless lacks provisions for a clear pathway back to the 'parent' node. This could lead to a common problem known as the 'getting lost in hyper-space syndrome' or the 'disorientation problem'. Nevertheless, as Bleber and Isakowitz (1995) correctly point out, until the development of the HDM, no formal data design model targeted for hypermedia applications existed. The emergence of the HDM is therefore a step in the right direction, and has influenced the design models that have since evolved (i.e. the OOHDM and the RMM design models).

## 3.14   THE OBJECT ORIENTED HYPERMEDIA DESIGN MODEL (OOHDM)

Developed by Schwabe and Rossi (1995) the OOHDM is an adaptation of the HDM and is based on an object oriented framework to allow concise description of complex information items as well as specification of complex navigational patterns and interface transformation. The OOHDM is the first model reviewed here that discusses the overall design and development process of hypermedia systems (Figure 3.8).

The main steps of the OOHDM are briefly explained below:

**Domain analysis:** A conceptual model of the application is built. At this stage the developer/designer will be modelling the semantics of the application domain

**Navigational analysis:** The navigational structure of hypermedia in terms of navigational contexts and classes such as nodes, links, etc. are defined.

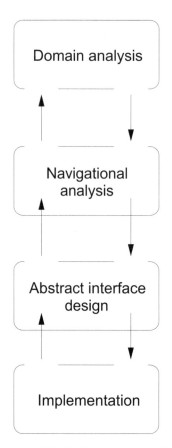

**Fig. 3.8**  The OOHDM Design Model (adapted from Schwabe and Rossi, 1995)

**Abstract interface design:** The abstract interface design defines the perceptual objects (e.g. pictures, a city map, etc.) in terms of interface classes (such as text fields and buttons).

**Implementation:** The implementation step maps interface objects to implementation objects and could also involve complex systems architecture (e.g. client server, sharing, etc.).

The OOHDM allows developers and designers of hypermedia systems to view the design process in a top down structured process, consisting of four steps, each of which is to focus on a particular design concern. OOHDM makes full use of abstraction and provides an opportunity for the systems to be built for future reuse, although the latter is barely addressed and the authors of the model themselves recognise the need to carry out further work in this area.

## 3.15   THE RELATIONSHIP MANAGEMENT METHODOLOGY (RMM)

Isakowitz, *et al.* (1995) proposed the 'Relationship Management Methodology' (RMM) based on their premise that hypermedia should be viewed as a vehicle for managing relationships among information objects. They noted that since hypermedia application design involves many different skill sets, the proposed design methodology should be able to cope with more than data models and systems level design issues. Figure 3.9 (Isakowitz, *et al.*, 1995) shows the RMM and its various parts.

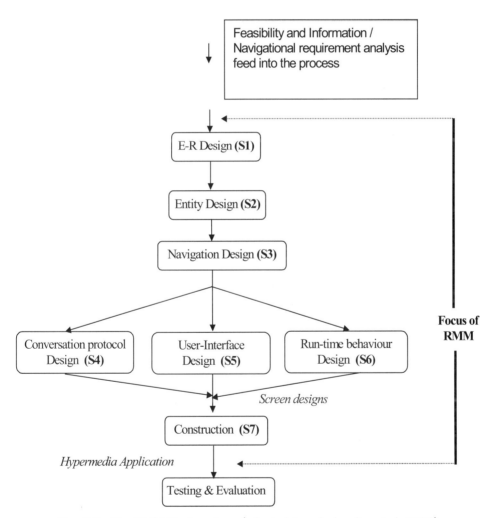

**Fig. 3.9**   The RMM Design steps (adapted from Isakowitz, *et al.*, 1995)

As can be seen, the RMM divides the process of design and implementation of hypermedia applications in the following seven steps:

**S1-E-R design:** Where the information domain of the application is represented. This stage of the design involves a study of relevant entities and the relationships of the application domain. These entities and applications form the basis of the hypermedia application.

**S2-Entity (slice) design:** This step determines how the information in the chosen entities is to be presented to the users, and how they may be accessed. It could involve splitting entities into meaningful slices and organising them into a hypertext network. In its simplest form all the information in an entity could be displayed within one window with scroll bars.

**S3-Navigational design:** This step deals with the design of the paths that will enable hypertext navigation.

**S4-Conversion protocol design:** Where a set of conversion rules are used to transform each element of the Data Model (Isakowitz, *et al.* 1995, propose a data model based on object orientation that they refer to as Relational Management Data Model – RMDM) into an object in the target platform.

**S5-User-Interface screen design:** This step involves the design of the screen layouts for every object appearing. This could include button layouts, appearance of nodes and location of navigational aids.

**S6-Run-Time behaviour design:** This step involves decisions about how links are traversed, backtracking as well as navigational mechanisms.

**S7-Construction:** The final step in the RMM is the construction and testing of the system.

The RMM is of particular importance as it tries to address the entire design and development process in developing hypermedia systems. The RMM addresses top-level design issues such as user-interface as well as the process of construction and evaluation of hypermedia packages. However, as can be seen from Figure 3.9 the RMM does not deal with feasibility, requirement analysis, and hardware and software tools. Since these elements affect the characteristic and behaviour of applications, the design model should deal with them.

# Chapter Summary

- The term hypertext implies a system that deals only with text. With the integration of sound and video technology into the desktop PC and the emergence of MM systems, the term hypermedia has been used for hypertext systems that are capable of linking together more than just textual information.
- It was not until the late 1980s, following 'Hypertext '87', that a general purpose design model for hypertext systems was proposed. This was mainly due to the lack of appropriate hardware and software development to allow large scale implementation of such systems.
- Amongst the key hypertext / hypermedia models that are discussed in the literature, one could name: Hypertext Abstract Machine (HAM), Dexter model, R-model, Tower model, CMIF multimedia model, Amsterdam Hypermedia Model (AHM), DeVise Hypermedia Model (DHM), Hypermedia Design Model (HDM), Object Oriented Hypermedia Design Model (OOHDM), and the Relationship Management Methodology (RMM) model.

# Exercises and Projects

### PROJECT

Write a report about the origin, concept and emergence of hypertext and hypermedia and present the information in a hypertext environment.

### RECALL QUESTIONS

1. With the aid of a diagram, discuss a typical hypertext system with its key components.
2. Discuss the different LINK structures that could exist within a hypertext environment.
3. Discuss the relationship between hypertext, hypermedia, and the WWW.
4. How would you relate Hypertext Abstract Machine to the architectural structure of the Internet and the WWW.
5. What are the key layers of Dexter's hypertext model?

6.     What are the key differences between the early hypertext models (like HAM and Dexter) and the later multimedia models like (AHM and DHM)?

7.     What are the key stages in multimedia design according the OOHDM model?

# Part II

## Multimedia Hardware, Software and Authoring Tools

*This section looks at multimedia hardware devices, multimedia enabling software, media integration issues and multimedia authoring tools.*

# 4

# Multimedia Hardware

*'The hope is that, in not too many years, human brain and computing machines will be coupled together very tightly and that the resulting partnership will think as no human brain has ever thought and process data in a way not approached by the information machines we know today.' Licklider (1960)*

## 4.1  INTRODUCTION

In Chapter 1 we discussed the emergence of multimedia PCs. The reader would recall that the initial multimedia PC was a 16 MHz machine with CD-ROM and limited audio, video capabilities. Technological innovation driven by market demands, over the last decade, have resulted in further advances in both multimedia hardware and software. Numerous devices and multimedia additions and enhancements are now available for both users and multimedia developers alike. This chapter will offer an overview of multimedia enabling peripherals that are used across both Mac and PC platforms.

## 4.2  STORAGE DEVICES

Multimedia content, i.e. audio, video, animation and graphics require massive storage space. A typical 15 seconds of video clip could take up as much as 15 MB of storage space in an uncompressed format, and therefore developing storage devices for multimedia systems has been one of the key areas of hardware development.

### 4.2.1  Hard Disk

While the early multimedia PC could offer a miserly 40 MB of storage capacity, the emerging systems are capable of thousands of MBs of storage which allows for more

**Fig. 4.1**    'Western Digital's' 120 GB drive

information as well as applications to be stored on desktop machines. While the basic mechanics of storage devices, particularly hard disk drives, have remained unchanged, nevertheless there has been marked improvements in terms of speed by which data could be accessed as well as their storage capacity.

Figure 4.1 shows one of the latest range of hard disk drives with 120 GB of capacity launched by 'Western Digital' one of the leading manufacturers of hard drives.

According to 10th edition of the Quantel Digital Fact Book (see www. quatel.com for more details), hard disk drives comprise of an assembly of up to 10 rigid platters coated with magnetic oxide, each capable of storing data on both sides. The magnetic recording surface has a read/write head, any one of which may be activated at a given instant. They can be written and read millions of times.

### 4.2.2    CD-ROM

CD-ROM (**C**ompact **D**isk – **R**ead **O**nly **M**emory) are optical disk devices capable of storing large amounts of data. CD-ROM is a rigid plastic disk that stores a large amount of data through the use of laser optics technology. Because they store data optically, CD-ROMs have a much higher memory capacity than computer disks that store data magnetically. The most common size for CD-ROM is 650 Megabytes. In another word a single CD-ROM has the storage capacity of nearly 600 floppy disks, enough to store more than 300,000 words of text. CD technology has advanced beyond read only and now there are CD read, write and re-write device (Figure 4.2).

There are different CD standards available which relate to the type of data that could be recorded on the CD. These are: *Red Book* used for audio CDs as well as data CDs, *Orange Book* format which is a format for recordable CDs and *White Book* a format for video CDs. CD devices are often referred to as either single or multi-session. A session on a CD includes a lead-in area, a program area (data or audio tracks) and a lead-out area therefore a multi-session disk is one, which has multiple sessions on one disk. Each session has its own lead-in, content and lead-out area, and is linked with other sessions. The speed at which a CD-ROM drive accesses informa-

**Fig. 4.2** Read and Write CD drive

tion from the disck is relative to the speed of the drive. A single speed CD-ROM drive (all the early versions of CD ROMs were single speed) reads data at around 150 K per second. Most CD-ROM drives in use at the moment are capable of 16, 32 and 50 speeds, which will read data at 2.4, 4.8 and around 8 megabytes per second respectively. CD write and rewrite devices are typically slower writing data and currently there are 12-speed write and re-writes CD drives around.

### 4.2.3 DVD

DVD, stands for **D**igital **V**ideo **D**isk. DVD is the next generation of optical disk storage technology, which is capable of storing more data, can hold cinema quality video, better-than-CD audio, and Giga bites of computer data. DVD technology is quickly replacing the old videotapes using VHS technology. The idea of DVD started in Hollywood where an *ad hoc* committee defined features for movies on 'CD' and it was in 1996 that the first DVD drive was sold in Japan.

Typically a DVD can hold 8 hours of high-quality video, or 30 hours of VHS quality video. Furthermore, DVD supports wide screen TV formats and it can handle up to 8 tracks of digital audio (for multiple languages). DVD format also offers a wide range of interactivity to users, including different interactive menus for option selection, different camera angles, instant replays and zooming facility. DVD is quickly becoming the storage standard for video formats and according to available statistics for the year 2000, more than 8.5 million DVD players were sold in US and UK had an installed customer base of more than 1 million users.

Both recordable (DVD-R) and re-writable (DVD-RAM) DVD discs have been developed. Recorders and disks for DVD-R have been available since 1997 but at a very high price. In August 2001, Hewlett-Packard announced plans to ship its first combination DVD + RW/CD-RW drive (Figure 4.3). Current DVD drives offer a lower capacity than read-only DVD discs. This limits their usefulness to applications where the full capacity of read-only DVD is not required. However, this capacity will increase to a full 4.7 GB per side.

**Fig. 4.3**   Hewlett-Packard's DVD writer the DVD 100I

Beside hard disk, CD-ROM and DVD drives there are a whole range of storage devices such as backup and ZIP drives that offer additional facilities for storing and backing data.

## 4.3   MULTIMEDIA INPUT AND OUTPUT DEVICES

While a multimedia system still requires traditional input and output devices such as a keyboard, mouse, monitor and a printer, there are now wide ranges of I/O devices, which add various functionalities to multimedia systems. These are:

- **Audio I/O devices** such as: audio add-on cards, MIDI interface (see Chapter 5 for more details on midi), and Speakers.
- **Video and Image devices** such as: video capture cards, scanners, digital cameras, digital camcorders, and virtual reality helmets, flat screen high-resolution monitors, multimedia data projectors.
- **Communication devices** such as: modems.

### 4.3.1   Audio I/O Devices

Audio input and output capability forms one of the key features of a multimedia system. A typical multimedia system would contain an audio add-on card which will provide the system with both input (minimum of two channels of sound input, e.g. microphone, electronic keyboard or midi-devices) and output capabilities (minimum two channels of output – e.g. speakers). An audio add-on card could take an analogue input such as a microphone and then digitise it for storage on the system. The digitised sound could then be manipulated, edited and incorporated into a multimedia application. Further discussion of sound editing and differences between digital and analogue sound formats is provided in Chapter 5.

### 4.3.2   Video and Image devices

Video and image devices are also one of the key components of a multimedia system. The technology as far as these types of devices are concerned has made significant advances. While early multimedia systems were only capable of outputting still images

**Fig. 4.4**  Samsungs' flat multimedia monitor with built-in speakers

of low resolution and low colour depth (typical 256 colour/8 bit) todays' multimedia system can output high resolution, true colour stills and moving images. New range of interactive monitors such as touch screens, which are particularly useful in the development of multimedia kiosks, have now emerged. New monitors have moved away from Cathode Ray Tube (CRT) technology to providing flat high-resolution 'flicker free' screens (Figure 4.4). Multimedia monitors also come with built-in speakers and high quality audio output. Key elements to consider when evaluating high quality monitors is firstly the monitor's resolution capability and secondly its refresh rates.

Refresh rate refers to the number of times the screen is re-drawn per second. A CDT (Colour Display Tube) monitor refreshes the identical display tens of times per second. It is also called the 'frequency rate' and measured in Hertz. For example a monitor with 60 Hz refresh frequency redraws the screen 60 times per seconds. This is, however, quite low and could look like a fluorescent light flickering. Typical multimedia monitors now are capable of 85 Hz and above refresh rates which provide users with flicker free viewing. Furthermore todays' monitors are capable of achieving very high resolutions. A typical high-resolution monitor would be capable of a Resolution of $1024 \times 768@85$ Hz or $1280 \times 1024@76$ Hz.

Another important image device for a multimedia system is a video capture card which allows multimedia designers to record and integrate digital video clips into their applications (Figure 4.5).

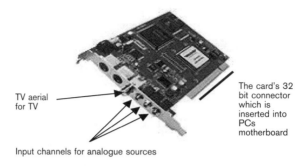

TV aerial
for TV

The card's 32
bit connector
which is
inserted into
PCs
motherboard

Input channels for analogue sources

**Fig. 4.5**  A typical video capture card

A video capture card is an add-on card, which is inserted into the mother-board of PC or Mac system. The card allows for analogue devices such as a video player, television or camcorder to act as an input device into the multimedia system. Most cards also come with a TV tuner built-in, which then allows for tuning and viewing of TV channels on your desktop PC. We will be reviewing video-editing software in Chapter 5. Other common multimedia devices used for inputting moving images into your desktop machine are digital camcorders and video conferencing cameras as well as some digital still image cameras that allow for a few seconds of video recordings. With the growth of the Internet and the World Wide Web, video conferencing has seen massive growth as a communication tool for companies. With the emergence of broadband Internet connections and the possibility of achieving decent data transfer rates delivering multimedia content across the world wide web is a practical possibility with wide reaching application areas (Figure 4.6).

A typical video conferencing package includes camcorders, video capture card and enabling software that would handle the transmission of video streams as well as receiving of video streams. Video conferencing relies heavily on the type of communication available. The standard end-user type of Internet connection such as 56 KB modem results in poor quality of sound and images as well as regular break of transmission. It is only through LAN (Local Area Network), ISDN, T1 and T3[1] type connections that practical video conferencing could be implemented.

Other video and image devices includes whole ranges of new digital still cameras as well as camcorders capable of recording high quality still and moving

---

[1]**ISDN** stands for **I**ntegrated **S**ervice **D**igital **N**etwork. ISDN is the digital telephone system that promised to standardize the high-speed (up to 128 Kbps) transmission of voice, data, and graphic images and replace the current slow analogue system. **T1/T3** refer to phone lines leased by big companies, universities, and the government for high-speed Net access and large-scale phone serices are called T1s or T3s, depending on the line's capacity. T1 lines, theoretically, carry data at a maximum 1.544 Mbps (bit-per-second) and T3 lines, are rated at 44 Mbps, which could easily handle the delivery of full-screen video.

**Fig. 4.6** Video Conferencing using laptop computers

SONY Glasstron PLM-A35E

**Fig. 4.7** Sonys' Glasstron virtual reality helmet (for more information you could check http://www.cybermind.nl/)

clips that are easily transferable into a multimedia application running either on PC or Mac.

Virtual reality equipment is another important multimedia enabling hardware that has emerged over the last decade. According to Aukstakalnis and Blatner (1992) 'Virtual Reality is a way for humans to visualise, manipulate and interact with computers and extremely complex data'. In order to create this virtual world as well as complex software that creates 3D virtual worlds the multimedia developers also requires special viewing devices called virtual reality helmets (Figure 4.7).

The virtual reality helmet or headset combines audio video and tracking capabilities to allow interaction with virtual world. The tracking system within a

**Fig. 4.8** Compaqs' latest mobile PC

virtual reality helmet or headset includes built-in sensors, which detects head movements in different directions including turning of the head to the right/left or up and down.

## 4.4   MOBILE MULTIMEDIA COMPUTING

The multimedia hardware technology is rapidly developing new devices, the buzzword here is convergence of technologies and the ideal is the multimedia user will end up with one device that is its web terminal, its CD-player, its television as well as its communication device (Figure 4.8).

A typical hand-held PC comes with 200 MHz above 32-bit Processor with 32 MB of Random Access Memory (RAM) or more and 16 MB of Read Only Memory (ROM). They come with touch screen monitors, which makes the interface much easier to handle. There also has been much improvement to the display of hand held devices. A typical palm top machine is equipped with colour reflective TFT[2] liquid crystal display for indoor and outdoor viewing and is capable of displaying 4,086 colours at a maximum resolution of 240 × 320 pixels, which provides a viewable image of around: 2.26 inches wide × 3.02 inches tall.

---

[2] Liquid Crystal Displays (LCDs) are non-emissive devices, which means that, they do not produce any form of light like a Cathode Ray Tube (CRT). Liquid Crystal LCDs either pass or block light that is reflected from an external light source or provided by a back/side lighting system. **TFT** (Thin-Film Transistor). A technology for building the LCD screens that is commonly found on laptop computers. TFT screens are brighter and more readable than dual-scan LCD screens, but consume more power and are generally more expensive.

The new range of hand-held devices or palm tops come with enough processing and storage power to run a wide range of applications. They offer connectivity to the WWW as well as being able to process multimedia content in a variety of formats, including audio and video.

Although the vision of a single hand-held multimedia machine still needs further clarification and the resolution of a number of technological issues, the emergence of palm devices and new range of 'media terminals' and 'communicators' (discussed briefly in Chapter 11) indicates that we are not far from realising this vision or at least a modified version of it.

## Chapter Summary

- Technological innovation driven by market demands, over the last decade, have resulted in further advances in both multimedia hardware and software.
- Compact Disk – Read Only Memory are optical disk devices capable of storing large amounts of data. A CD-ROM is a rigid plastic disk that stores a large amount of data through the use of laser optics technology.
- Digital Video Disk. DVD is the next generation of optical disk storage technology, which is capable of storing more data, can hold cinema quality video, better-than-CD audio, and Giga bites of computer data.
- While a multimedia system still requires traditional input and output devices such as a keyboard, mouse, monitor and a printer, there is now a wide range of I/O devices, which add various functionalities to multimedia systems. These are: Audio I/O devices and Video and Image devices.
- Virtual reality equipment is another important multimedia enabling hardware that has emerged over the last decade.

## Exercises and Projects

**PROJECT**

- Carry out research on the range of multimedia hardware devices that could be used in delivering multimedia content on both the World Wide Web and CD-ROM environment. Your report should also cover the impact of the new mobile multimedia devices such as palm tops and mobile communicators.

## RECALL QUESTIONS

1.   What are the differences between CD-ROM and DVD technologies?
2.   Video conferencing relies heavily on the type of communication channels available; which of the following types of connection would be more suitable and why? ISDN, T1 or T3.
3.   What are the differences between LCD, CRT, TFT and CDT?
4.   What are the different CD standards available and what do they relate to?
5.   Discuss what hardware and software tools you require to include digital audio within your multimedia applications.
6.   Discuss what hardware and software tools you require to include digital video within your multimedia applications.

# 5

# Multimedia Enabling Software and Media Integration Issues

*'An issue that arises frequently is identifying the best way of producing multimedia programmes. Our students and developers like clear recipes or prescription: how much text, what size, which colour, how many pictures, for what purpose...They feel some kind of multimedia illiteracy but I am not sure if we can currently speak of 'multimedia syntax' as we could speak of visual literacy...' Bartolome and Sandals (1996)*

## 5.1 INTRODUCTION

In parallel to the development of multimedia hardware, there have been significant advances in multimedia enabling software. We only need to look back some fifteen years to realise that most desktop machines (with the exception of Apple Mac) were using text-based operating systems with very little multimedia functionality. Microsofts' Disk Operating System (DOS), the predecessor to the current Windows operating system had virtually no multimedia capability. Compare that with the latest version of Windows operating system the XP, with more emphasis on multimedia content delivery clearly illustrates the significance and effects of multimedia technology on desktop computing operating environment. Inclusion of multimedia applications such as the '*Movie Maker*' and tools to create both audio and data CDs are but a few examples. The same applies to the latest version of Apples' operating systems (version X) that contains a wide range of multimedia enabling software tools. The rapid development of multimedia operating environments has been matched with the development of software tools. These could be categorised as:

- Image creation, preparation and editing tools;
- Audio preparation and editing tools;
- Video preparation and editing tools;
- Animation tools;
- 3D tools; and
- Multimedia authoring tools (discussed in Chapter 6).

These tools are used for various media creation and preparation activity. While the multimedia production process would not have succeeded without the right tools it is also crucial to have an in-depth understanding of how text, graphic, audio and video could seamlessly be integrated together. It is therefore not hard to deduct that the multimedia designer and developer is no longer a 'programmer' in the classic software engineering model but a producer that requires knowledge and understanding of various issues and elements that make the multimedia project.

In order to get the reader more familiar with the key multimedia elements the following discussion on media elements are presented before an overview of various multimedia enabling software.


## 5.2    TEXT

Text forms an important part of any multimedia package. Depending what the application is for, the use of text could vary. For example, an action arcade type of game may require very little text while a multimedia encyclopedia will require enormous amount of text. Therefore the correct presentation of textual information in different typefaces and in harmony with other media elements is an important part of the design process.

There are generally two groups of fonts or typefaces: serif and sans serif. The key difference between these two groups is the sharper angular edge of the serif family as compare to the straight edges of the sans-serif family. Here are some examples of the two different groups.

Beside the two groups of fonts, various desktop publishing packages come with different types of typefaces that could be used within a multimedia application. It is also possible to manipulate the text to create 3D. Here is an example of 'word art' created on Word for Windows.

Additionally there are font creation packages (like fontograph) that would allow the multimedia designer to create specific typefaces including typefaces for other languages or special symbols (see Figure 5.3).

In summary the issues that the multimedia designer needs to take into account while integrating text includes:

- Different fonts look different on various platforms.

| Examples of Serif Types of Fonts | Examples of Sans Serif Types of Fonts |
|---|---|
| **Times New Roman**<br>**Palatino**<br>**Book Antiqua**<br>**Rock Well** | **Arial**<br>**Lucida Sans**<br>Berlin Sans FB<br>Comic Sans MS |

**Fig. 5.1** Different families of typefaces

**Fig. 5.2** An Example of a 'Word Art'

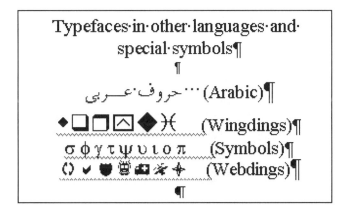

**Fig. 5.3** Special symbols and non-English typeface

- Use of special type of fonts require set-up provisions on the clients machine, and the
- Need to strike a right balance between text size, colour and special effects like anti-alias, where the text is gently blended into the background.

## 5.3   WORKING WITH GRAPHICS

Still images and graphics are also crucial in developing interactive multimedia applications. Working with graphics requires knowledge and expertise in terms of both creating them and being able to manipulate them using tools to add various effects. Different types of graphic packages create different types of files. Fortunately most current multimedia authoring tools are capable of importing and exporting graphic files in a variety of formats therefore allowing the designer to explore different file formats for different application requirements.

In general graphic files are divided up into three groups:

- Colour graphics: including 4 bit graphic – i.e. 16 colours; 8 bit, 256 colours; 16 bit, 32,768 colours; 24 and 32 bit graphic files capable of true colour representation (i.e. millions of colours).
- Gray Scale Graphics: graphic files that are effectively in black and white but capable of displaying various depth (4 bit, 8 bit, 16 bit) shade of gray, and
- Mono Graphics: black and white colour only.

The multimedia designer also ought to be familiar with different graphic file formats. Some of the key formats are:

**.PICT:** The default Apple Mac graphic file format, which is available to any graphic application running on an Apple Mac platform. The key characteristic of a PICT type of file is its ability to contain both the bitmap as well as the vector drawn objects in the some graphic.

**.BMP:** Windows default file format. BMP format supports RGB, Indexed Colour, Grayscale, and Bitmap colour modes, does not support alpha channels.

**JPEG (.JPG):** Stands for Joint Photographic Experts Group which was responsible for the development of the image mapping format and standards used widely across the world. JPG is a compressed graphic file format used to display photographs and other continuous-tone images and can handle various colour depths. JPG is the most popular file format used on the Web. As JPEG files are compressed the file sizes are typically small and therefore suitable for use on the Web. Most graphic applications allow the designer to select the degree of compression of a JPG file by indicating low, medium or high-resolution output settings. A JPEG image is automatically decompressed when opened.

**.GIF:** CompuServes' Graphic Interchange File format is also a compressed file format developed by CompuServe for use over the Internet. In order to keep file size down a GIF file could only handle 16 bit colour depths (i.e. 256 colours). GIF format preserves transparency in indexed-colour images and allows the designer to create small-animated images by placing images on top of each other. All current versions of Web browsers are capable of viewing and displaying these types of files.

**.TIFF:** : Tagged Interchange File Format is an uncompressed file format that is commonly used in desktop publishing packages and is the favourite file format with printing companies. The strength of the TIFF format is that it's flexible bitmap image format is supported by virtually all paint, image editing, and page-layout applications.

**.EPS:** Encapsulated PostScript language file format used in PhotoShop can contain both vector and bitmap graphics and is supported by a wide range of graphic, illustration, and page-layout programs. EPS format is used to transfer PostScript-language artwork between applications. When an EPS file containing vector graphics is opened, image manipulation software like PhotoShop rasterizes the image, converting the vector graphics to pixels.

**.PSD:** is the format used by PhotoShop to save newly created or manipulated files. PSD supports all available image modes (Bitmap, Greyscale, Indexed Colour, RGB, CMYK, Lab, and Multi-Channel). PSD file are not compressed and contain information about various graphic layers that could exist within a file.

**.PNG:** Portable Network Graphics was developed as a patent-free alternative to GIF. PNG is also a compressed file format for display of images on the World Wide Web. Unlike GIF, PNG is capable of displaying 24-bit images and produces background transparency. The problem with PNG file is that unlike GIF files that are supported by all Web browsers some Web browsers do not support PNG images.

**Graphic package Specific file formats:** beside the above file formats there are also different file formats created by different file packages. For example Macromedias, FreeHand creates file with **.FH8** (for FreeHand version 8) extensions or CorelDraw creates file with **.CDR** extension and so on.

A good multimedia designer would typically work with a variety of formats. For example, creating the initial graphics may by done in PhotoShop (which creates large size files) and then exported into a JPG format for integration into the multimedia application.

## 5.4   WORKING WITH SOUND

The introduction of audio capability into Desktop PC added powerful new function-ality that could be exploited developing interactive and multimedia packages. Recording, editing and playing back audio files is an area that requires in-depth knowledge of digital audio and quite often big multimedia projects usually have a sound engineer advising the development team.

There are two general types of audio files, which could be incorporated into a multimedia environment:

1.   MIDI files
2.   Digitized Sound

**1. MIDI Files (Musical Instrument Digital Interface MIDI):** was developed in 1980s as a set of communication protocols allowing music and sound synthesizers from different manufacturers to communicate with each other. MIDI allowed any instru-ment with a suitable five-pin MIDI socket to communicate with any other instrument, whatever the manufacturer. A MIDI type file contains no sound but rather provides a protocol for passing detailed descriptions of a musical score, such as notes and what instrument will play these notes. As MIDI files contain no actual digitized audio they are up to a 1000 smaller than a typical digital audio file containing digital sound information.

The introduction of MIDI communication protocol and the emergence of sequencer software in the 1980s meant that musicians and non-musicians alike could make music with ease. A sequencer is best explained as a kind of word processor for music. It allows the developer to enter the notes or play them in from a suitable keyboard and, like a word processor, it enables the developer to make changes to existing files or documents very simply. The diversity of MIDI instruments and even standards towards the late 80s and early 90s prompted several manufacturers to get together and try to produce the framework for a standard which became know as General MIDI. The General MIDI set the standard for the name and type of sounds and also the location these sounds could be called from. For example, in a General MIDI instrument, you'll always find the piano in location number one. General MIDI, however, had a lot of limitation in terms of editing existing MIDI files and hence limited creativity in terms of creating audio files of very high quality, that matched the original sound intended by the composer. In the early 1990s Yamaha, one of the key players in keyboards and computer based sequencing applications introduced the XG format as a kind of superset of General MIDI. Towards the end of the 1990s Yamaha introduced the XF file format which expands the capability of General MIDI and XG without sacrificing the compatibility afforded by those systems. According to Yamaha the XF is designed to take advantage of the increased potential of new Yamaha

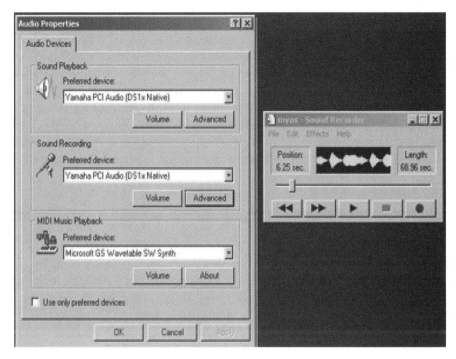

**Fig. 5.4**   Windows sound recording software with Audio Properties window

keyboards and computer-based sequencing applications. The XF format could include important details of a song including the title, author and composer, the songs lyrics, copyright information or even the musical style enabling searching and categorisation of songs.

**2. Digitized Sound:**   Digital sound could be created from a microphone, a synthesizer, CD player or even from a TV broadcast. In contrast to MIDI data, digital audio is the actual representation of sound, stored in the forms of thousands of individual numbers called 'samples'.

For best quality of sound play-back i.e. CD-quality you require a 44 KHz (kilohertz) sampling rate, 16 bit resolution, Stereo which creates very large '.wav' files. A typical 1-minute CD-quality audio requires around 10.5 MB of space. If the same file is sampled at 5.5 KHz sampling rate, 8-bit resolution and mono recording the file size for 1 minute of digital sound will reduce to typically 325 KB. Typical digital file format for Windows environment is **.wav**, which is the Waveform file interchange. The .wav format includes no compression and therefore the file size created is quite large and typically not suitable for use on the WWW.

The **.AIFF** (Audio Interchange File Format) is the native audio file format for Apple Mac environment and its characteristics are very similar to **.wav** files.

Towards the end of 1980s attempts were made to introduce portable audio compression formats that would result in smaller audio files. MPEG (Motion Picture Experts Group) layer 1, 2 and layer 3 commonly known as MP3 are the result of these attempts. MP3 format works on the basis of the fact that the human hearing range is between 20 Hz to 20 Khz and it is most sensitive between 2 to 4 KHz. Hence the MP3 compression deletes the 'redundant' information that human hearing could not pick up, reducing the file size of a typical digital audio by up to 12 times. MP3 is currently the most commonly used format to download and deliver audio files over the World Wide Web and is quickly becoming the audio standard for the delivery of audio over the net.

## 5.5   WORKING WITH VIDEO

Introduction of video, which could be defined as seamless integration of moving images and synchronized audio, created interesting possibilities in developing media rich multimedia applications. Carefully planned, well-executed and appropriate video clips can make a dramatic difference to a multimedia project.

Creating Digital video requires professional tools editing facilities and large storage space. Creating digital video on a desktop PC requires a video capture card and an appropriate video authoring tool such as Adobe Premier (discussed in more detail later on in this chapter).

There are different video standards and formats, which include:

- **NTSC** (National Television Standards Committee) developed in the 1950s which defines a video standard made up of 525 horizontal scan lines drawn every 1/30 of a second. This is a standard used mainly in USA, Japan.
- **PAL** (Phase Alternate Line) is a set of standards used in Britain, Europe, and some other countries. According to Vaughan (1994) this is an integrated method of adding colour to a black and white television signal that paints 625 lines at a frame rate of 25 Fps, each taking 1/50 of second to draw (50 Hz).
- There are also other standards including **SECAM** (Sequential Colour and Memory system) used in France.
- **HDTV** (High definition TV) is the new standard in television technology, which provides wide-screen picture quality similar to 35 mm film along with compact disc (CD) sound quality. HDTV offers wider pictures with greater detail and the clarity of motion pictures. Compared to standard television (NTSC, PAL or SCAM), the HDTV is wider with higher aspect ratio. While standard television typically has an aspect ratio of 4:3 (four units wide, three units high) the HDTV aspect ratio is 16:9. The key difference between old standards and the HDTV is the high resolution of HDTV comprising of 1080 active lines (1125 total) whereas current standard television pictures are composed of only 486 active lines (525 total).

Another important issue in working with video is the different type of file formats for digital video integration into multimedia applications. The key file formats that the reader needs to be aware of are:

- **.AVI** (Audio Video Interleaved) – also called Video for Windows (VFW) is one of the most popular formats for presenting video. This format was developed by Microsoft and is the native digital file format on a PC environment.
- **QuickTime** is a digital video format developed and supported primarily by Apple computers but can be viewed on practically every platform available today. QuickTime was one of the first digital video formats to be developed. Quick-Time is very similar to AVI but provides better quality output. QuickTime produces files with extensions .mov, movie, or qt.
- **.MPEG** (Moving Pictures Experts Group): Founded in 1988 the groups task was to create standards for digital video (sequences of images in time) and audio compression. The idea behind MPEG video compression is to remove spatial redundancy within a video frame and temporal redundancy between video. This could result in up to 30 times compression and hence greatly reduced video file sizes.

With the emergence of the WWW there are further developments in terms of audio and video delivery over the net, particularly streaming technology, which is discussed in Chapter 11.

## 5.6    IMAGE CREATION AND PREPARATION TOOLS

Having discussed media elements and some media integration issues it is useful to introduce the reader to some key multimedia enabling software that could be used in media creation and preparation of multimedia projects. With the emergence of multi-media, one could see the growing number of software tools that are available to the designer and developer of the multimedia systems.

These tools are a vital part of any design and development activity and therefore need to be carefully chosen. It is also clear we all have our favourite set of tools that we work with. Having worked with different software graphic packages it is quite clear to me that as far as range of functionalities are concerned the leading software tools are similar.

The key issue is to understand the concepts and methods behind creating a piece of graphic. For the purpose of this book I will briefly cover two different sets of tools that could be used in both creation of graphics as well as manipulation of scanned or already made images. For graphic creation I will be reviewing Macro-media's Freehand (Current version 10) and for image manipulation, Adobe's PhotoShop (Current version 6).

Selection tool that is used for selection and resizing.

Rectangle tool to draw rectangles or squares.

Draws ellipses and circles.

Draws freeform and curved freeform paths.

Freeform tool, which is used, to push or pull any part of the path.

Cut tool cuts a selected area.

Rotation tools that rotates a selected object around a fixed point.

Scale tool that is used in enlarging or reducing graphics.

Text tool to insert a text block.

Polygon tool to draw polygons or stars.

Draws a line, which consists of two points.

Pen tool, which draws paths by placing curve, corner, and connector points.

The Bezigon tool draws straight lines and arcs.

Reflection tool that flips a selected object horizontally or vertically.

Skew tool that slants an object at an angle.

Tracing tools which could trace any image in Freehand environment.

Freehand's zoom tools which allows magnifying of images.

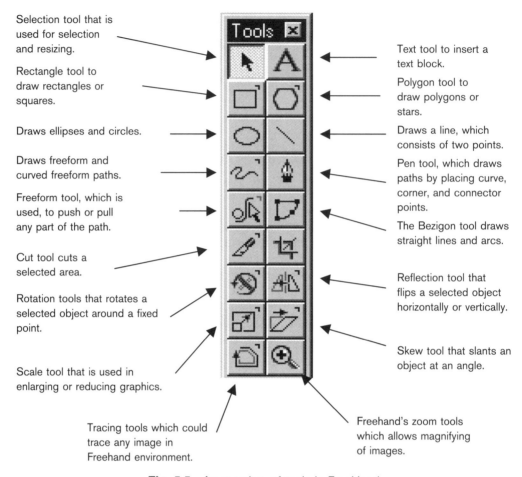

**Fig. 5.5** An overview of tools in FreeHand

### 5.6.1 Creating Graphics

Most graphic creation packages come with a set of tools that could be viewed as the paintbrush and paint of the painter allowing the designer to start the process of creating a new drawing.

One of the key concepts that the reader needs to become familiar with is the idea of creating various layers within a single drawing. Layering allows for the creation of complex images superimposed on each other. Most graphic creation tools, including FreeHand, also allow text manipulation and special effects, which could include anti-alias, text shadowing, and text skewing.

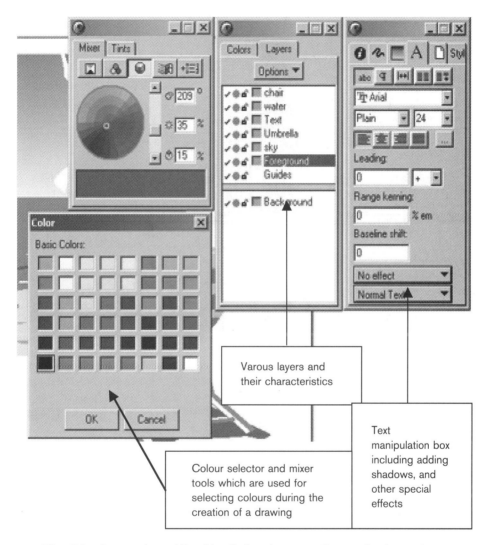

**Fig. 5.6** An overview of FreeHand's layering, text effect and colour selector

### 5.6.2 Image Manipulation Tools

One of the leading image manipulation tools available in the market is Adobe's PhotoShop. An image manipulation tool is typically used in order to create complex effects on scanned images or graphics created in other packages.

Like FreeHand, PhotoShop also comes with a set of tools that allows the designer to manipulate the image. Like FreeHand, PhotoShop also allows complex manipulation using layering and various filtering techniques (Figure 5.8).

The marquee tool which allows rectangular, and elliptical, selections.

The lasso tools which allows freehand and polygonal selections.

Crop and slice tools.

Airbrush and cloning tools. Cloning tool paints with a sample of an image paints.

The blur tool which is used to blur hard edges in an image.

Pen tool, which is used, draws smooth-edged paths.

Annotation tools which allows adding voice notations to an image.

The move tool moves selections, layers.

The magic wand tool which selects similarly coloured areas.

Paint bucket used for colouring a selected area.

Text tool to insert a text block.

Line tool which allows drawing of 2D shapes such as line, rectangle...etc.

Eye drop tool which allows the sampling of colours in an image.

Zooming tool.

Foreground and background colour selector.

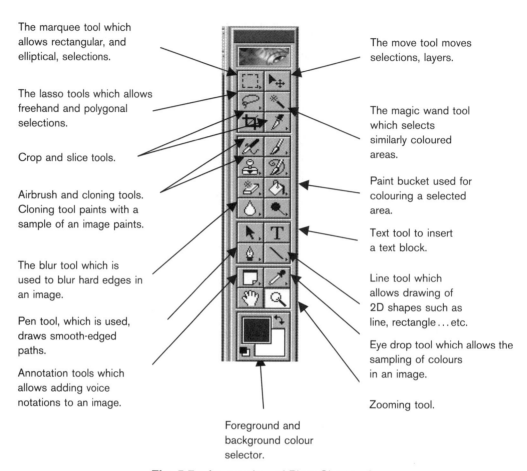

**Fig. 5.7** An overview of PhotoShop tools

### 5.6.2.1 Creative Imaging With PhotoShop

Let us look at some examples used in the development of the interactive multimedia systems reviewed in the case studied presented in Chapter 9.

### Creating a Background Image and a Menu Structure

To create a background image with menu structure, the first step is to determine the size of the image you are creating. This is usually done in the new file set-up section. As can be seen from Figure 5.9 the new file option allows the designer to set width, height, resolution, mode (i.e. greyscale, RGB, index...etc.) as well as transparency settings for the image background. In this particular example we have chosen $640 \times 480$ resolution to cover the entire screen. The steps to create the background image are illustrated in Table 5.1.

And the final result is shown in Figure 5.10.

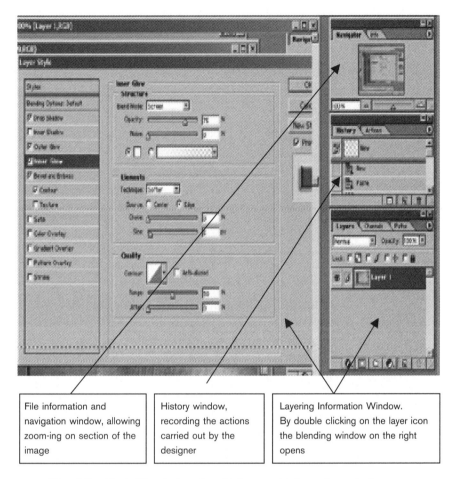

| File information and navigation window, allowing zoom-ing on section of the image | History window, recording the actions carried out by the designer | Layering Information Window. By double clicking on the layer icon the blending window on the right opens |

**Fig. 5.8**   PhotoShop's layering, history and information windows

### *Image and Photo Manipulation*

Another very powerful feature in PhotoShop is the range of options that the designer has in manipulating scanned photographs. Table 5.2 illustrates some of these functionalities.

## 5.7   3D IMAGES AND ANIMATION TOOLS

Animation and 3D graphics adds visual impact to a multimedia project. But creating animation requires an in-depth knowledge of 2D and 3D graphics and image manipulation techniques.

**Fig. 5.9** PhotoShop's new file options

**Fig. 5.10** The BRM Menu (see Chapter 9) created using PhotoShop

According to Vaughan (1994) animation is possible because of a biological phenomenon known as *persistence vision*. This means that an object seen by the human eye remains mapped on the eye's retina for a brief time after viewing, hence making it possible for a series of images changing very slightly to seemingly blend together to create an illusion of movement. Persistence of vision was discovered in the 1800s. This led to invention of devices such as the zoetrope. The zoetrope was a cylindrical device, which rotated on its axis of symmetry (Figure 5.11).

1. Starting with a paint bucket and painting the background blue.

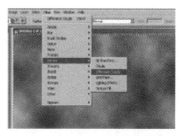

2. Using the filters menu, we choose Render option and then select Difference Clouds to create a nice 3D painting effect.

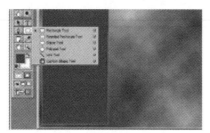

3. Using the rectangle tool from the tool bar we can create a blue bar in the left hand side.

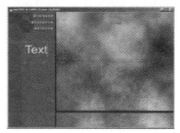

4. Using the text tool from the tool bar the title is added to the blue bar.

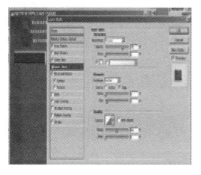

5. To create the menu buttons, we use the rectangle tool from the tool bar and create a blue horizontal bar, then by double clicking on this layer on the layers window we create shadow, inner and outer glow, emboss and bevel effects for the button.

6. Using the text tool we type option 1 on the 3D button we have created and again using the blending option (by double clicking on the layer) we add shadow text and other effects. This process is repeated to created the other buttons for our menu.

**Table 5.1** Steps to create the background images using PhotoShop

1. Initial scanned image.

2. Image brightness and contrast adjusted using image menu and then selecting the contrast option.

3. Scanned Image equalised and ready for some 'Arty' effects.

4. Using Filters menu to add texturing effect to the Photo results in a natural painting texture.

5. Using Filter menu and Render option to add lighting effects.

6. Again using the Filter menu and the Distort option to create a wave effect.

**Table 5.2**   Image manipulation using PhotoShop

**Fig. 5.11** A picture of Zoetrope from the Web pages of London Museum (http://www.londonmuseum.org.uk)

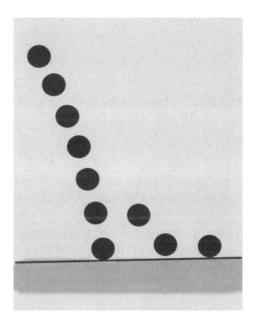

**Fig. 5.12** Simple animation sequence of a bouncing ball

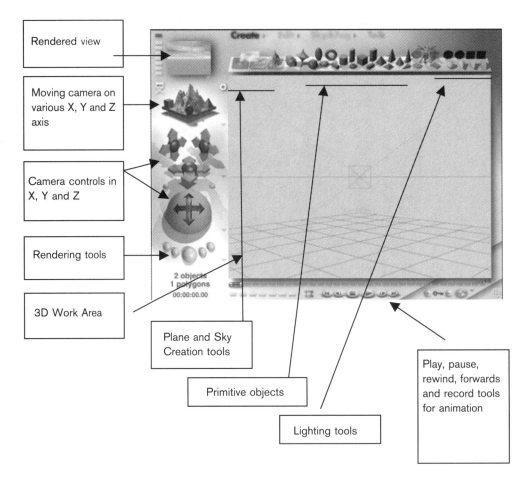

**Fig. 5.13** Overview of Tools in Corel Bryce 4

Animation and 3D tools are highly specialized and often quite expensive to obtain. To understand the 3D image creation process the multimedia designer is required to understand working with X, Y and Z planes, to be able to understand keyframing and wireframes concepts and have knowledge of rendering techniques using material libraries. The simple principle of animation could be defined, as creating a sequence of images that are related to each other and once put together will display a continuous sequence of events. An illustration of this can be seen in Figure 5.12 showing a simple animation sequence of a ball falling and then slightly bouncing up from the floor.

There are a number of useful tools available for animation and 3D graphics, including 3D Studio by AutoDesk and Corel Bryce 4.

**Fig. 5.14** Bryce material library

Unlike traditional 2D graphic packages, 3D tools don't have the 'usual' tool bar icons we can find in PhotoShop or Freehand. Bryce's interface is shown in Figure 5.13.

Let us look at an example using Corel Bryce 4. First using the plane and sky tools we create the plane and sky wireframes. These could be then be rendered using the predefined material library. The material library allows the designer to select the texture of the wireframe, which is then filled-in using the rendering process (Figure 5.14).

Using the object primitives, the terrain and sky labs, we could place objects on the desktop and determine their relationships together. Once every object is placed, and once we have chosen the appropriate lighting, material and camera angle the image could be rendered. Figure 5.15 shows the wireframe and then the rendered version of the image.

To create an animation sequence the designer could manipulate various camera angles, zooming in and out, as well as adding other images and then using the recording facility to create the sequence. Animation and 3D graphics are becoming more and more popular on the WWW. Animation created on Macromedia Flash (see Chapter 11 for more details) have transformed the Web from its original hypertext character into a truly hypermedia environment where media rich information is presented to the users in variety of formats.

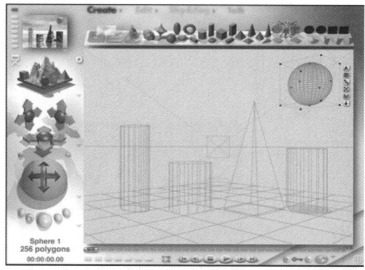

**Fig. 5.15** The wireframe image before and after rendering

## 5.8    AUDIO EDITING AND CREATION TOOLS

Windows and Apple operating systems come equipped with basic audio recording software, which enables the multimedia designer to plug in any analogue source (i.e. microphone) into the desktop machine sound card and start recording digital audio. Furthermore, the audio the recording software could also record directly from an audio CD playing on CD-ROM or DVD player. Other sources of audio could be

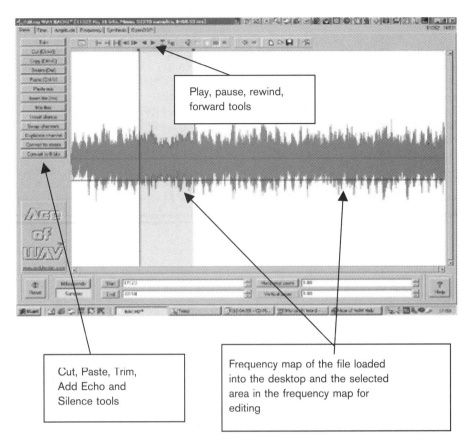

Play, pause, rewind, forward tools

Cut, Paste, Trim, Add Echo and Silence tools

Frequency map of the file loaded into the desktop and the selected area in the frequency map for editing

**Fig. 5.16**   AceofWave editing desktop

file downloads from the World Wide Web. Sound editing like animation requires in-depth understanding of how sound editors work and various technical issues regarding reducing noise interference, amplitude and pitch settings, and balancing the output. Sound editors also allow the multimedia designer to create echoes, pauses, and fade in the sound. Sound amplification and getting ride of unwanted noise is also possible. Most sound editing tools like SoundForg, WaveEdit or AceofWave come with work area where a frequency map of the recorded audio is presented to the user for editing and manipulation (Figure 5.16).

Digital audio files require large storage space if not compressed.

Audio file sizes are dependent on sampling rate and whether the sound is mono or stereo. Table 5.3, shows approximate file sizes on various settings

Amongst the audio settings available in various sound editing tools that the multimedia designer ought to be familiar with are:

| Channels | Bit depth | Sampling rate | Appx. file size | Quality/Use |
|----------|-----------|---------------|-----------------|-------------|
| Stereo | 16 bit* | 44 KHz | 10 MB | CD Audio Stereo |
| Mono | 16 bit | 44 KHz | 5 MB | Voice over |
| Stereo | 8 bit | 44 KHz | 5 MB | Voice over |
| Mono | 8 bit | 44 KHz | 2.5 MB | Voice over |
| Stereo | 16 bit | 22 KHz | 2.5 MB | FM Radio |
| Mono | 8 bit | 22 KHz | 1.3 MB | FM Radio |
| Mono | 8 bit | 11 Khz | 600 KB | Telephone |
| Mono | 8 bit | 5.5 Khz | 300 KB | Poor Telephone |

* New sound editing tools like sound Forge version 5 allow 24 bit integer and 32 bit floating bit depths for sound recordings

**Table 5.3**   Approximate file sizes on various audio settings

- **Volume settings:** allowing increase or decrease of an audio file.
- **Silence settings:** adding and removing silence from an audio file.
- **Switching channels:** changing an audio file from mono to stereo or vice versa.
- **Normalisation:** normalises the loudness of an audio file.
- **Switching bit depth:** changing the bit depth of an audio file. For example changing an 8 bit clip to 16 or 24 bit file.
- **Fade In/Out:** allows fading in the sound, i.e. there is a smooth transition at the beginning of the file rather than an abrupt start. Fading out does the same and fades the sound out towards the end of the file.
- **Reverse settings:** allows the reversal of a recorded audio file, which could create interesting effects particularly on voice over.
- **Digital Signal Processing:** allows advance manipulation of recorded sound in terms of reverberation, chorus, flange and other special effects.
- **Distortion settings:** allows for distortions, audio signals and other effects to be introduced into the audio file.
- **Delay settings:** allows delays to be added at any arbitrary point in the recorded audio file.
- **Pan settings:** which is used to control the position of the sound between the right and left channels.

## 5.9   VIDEO EDITING AND CREATION TOOLS

The integration of digital video into desktop PC like the introduction of audio opened enormous possibilities to add media rich content to the multimedia applications. The integration of video into multimedia applications firstly requires a video capture card

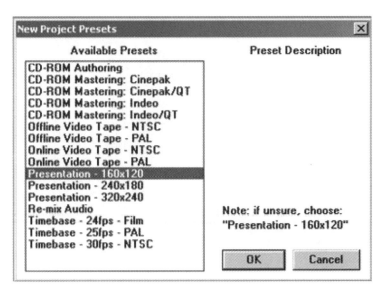

**Fig. 5.17** A View of Adobe Premier's opening screen

that can communicate and read the video analogue sources and secondly some capture and editing software to store the digital file. Video like traditional film is a set of still images shown at a set frequency for example 30 still images per seconds. Like animation the view of moving images by the human eye is due to the *persistence of vision* discussed earlier in this chapter. A motion picture camera used in creating big screen movies captures images at a rate of 24 frames per second.

Tannenbaum (1998) points out that there are three basic stages in the use of moving images in an interactive multimedia application: capturing, editing and presentation. In order to carry out these basic tasks there are different software tools available. Depending on the complexity of the tool and the range of functionalities offered they could be very expensive. Professional video clips require studio conditions and professional camera and sound engineers and it is often the case that in large multimedia projects this part of the project is contracted out to professional film studios. Most video capture cards also provide some basic software that could be used for capturing and storing of the digital video. Video for Windows and Apples QuickTime were one of the first video tools available on Apple and Windows environment. For a more professional result Adobe Premier offers a wide range of options and functionalities. When first starting the programme, the user is asked to indicate the size of the presentation they are creating (see Figure 5.17).

The first step is to capture the video clip. Adobe Premier comes with a utility called capture which captures a video clip based on user defined settings. This requires a lot of computing power and hard disk speed and storage space. If the computing

**Fig. 5.18**  Video clip opened in Adobe Premier

power is not sufficient the software will start dropping frames and the output could be a very jagged clip with audio and video occasionally out of sync. Once the video clip is captured it could be opened in Adobe Premier as a file which then could be edited or manipulated (see Figure 5.18).

Once a clip is imported it can be placed (by dragging and pasting) in Premier's work area. This process divides the video clip into its individual still images and its audio content (see Figure 5.19).

Once a clip is divided into still images then its possible to create transition effects for various images, add text or graphics over a certain image and create special effects (Figure 5.20).

Finally once all the editing and special effects are done, we need to put the clip back together. Going to *Make* menu and then selecting *Make Movie* starts the processing of creating a new movie clip. When creating a new movie clip it is necessary to make a number on important decisions.

Firstly what video format should the output have (i.e. AVI, MOV or MPG)? Secondly the size and resolution of the output, the larger the size the bigger the size of the outfile. Thirdly you need to decide to synchronise and integrate the audio into your clip. Premier allows the designer to change the characteristics of the audio by changing its bit depth and its sampling rate.

Figure 5.21 illustrates the make movie option.

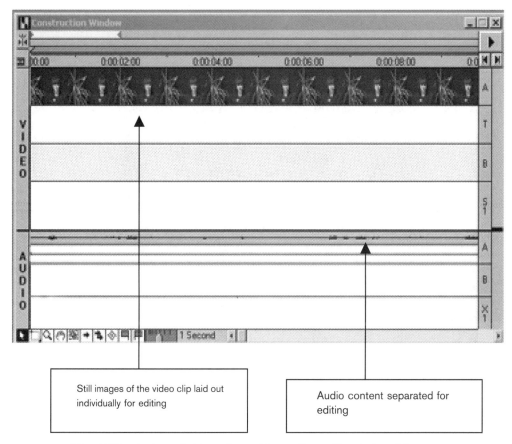

Still images of the video clip laid out individually for editing

Audio content separated for editing

**Fig. 5.19**    A view of video clip and its audio on Premier's editing area

Other important issues that require attention are the use of compression to create the new clip. The compression options provide the user with various options including the type of compression used as well as setting the number of frames per second (Figure 5.22).

Amongst the format and compression options MPG provides the best quality and the smallest file size.

The emergence of the WWW and the gradual improvements in the bandwidth, particularly the introduction of broadband has meant that delivery of audio and video over the Web is now a real possibility, chapter 11 will look at how streaming technology and tools associated with it is delivering media rich content over the internet.

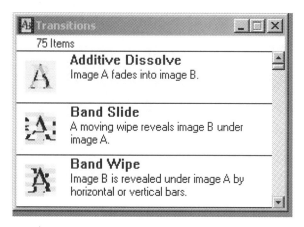

**Fig. 5.20**  Adobe Premier's transition window

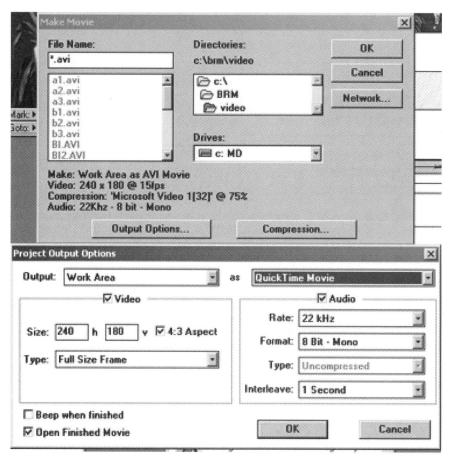

**Fig. 5.21**  A view of make movie option with output options selected

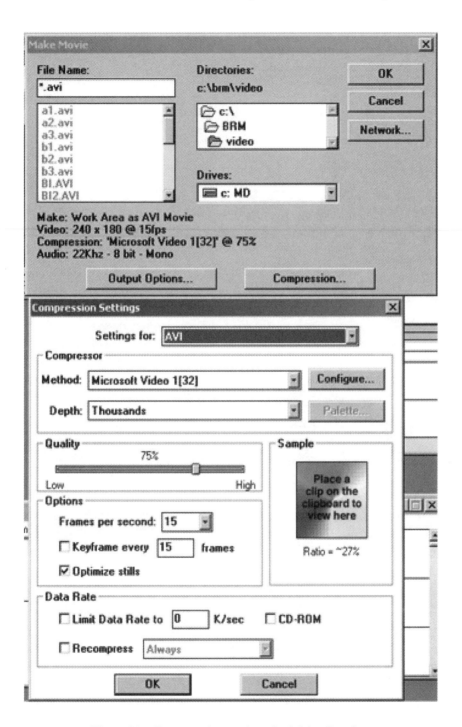

**Fig. 5.22**  Compression settings in Adobe Premier

# Chapter Summary

- The rapid development of multimedia operating environments has been matched with the development of software tools. These could be categorised as:
  - Image creation, preparation and editing tools:
    e.g. FreeHand, PhotoShop, Corel Draw, etc.
  - Audio preparation and editing tools:
    e.g. SoundForge, AceofWave, etc.
  - Video preparation and editing tools:
    e.g. Adobe Premier.
  - Animation tools:
    e.g. 3D Studio, Corel Bryce and Flash
  - 3D tools:
    e.g. Corel Bryce
  - Multimedia authoring tools:
    e.g. Macromedia Director, Authorware, etc.
- These tools are vital part of any design and development activity and therefore need to be carefully chosen. It is also clear we all have our favourite set of tools that we work with. Having worked with different software graphic packages it is quite clear to me that as far as range of functionalities are concerned the leading software tools are similar.

# Exercises and Projects

## PROJECT

- A marketing company wants to develop a corporate image CD-ROM for a Blue Chip client. The company approaches you as a Multimedia designer/consultant to seek advice on the range of tools and techniques available in creating such a CD. You need to produce an executive report outlining your suggestions about the technology involved and the expertise requires.

## RECALL QUESTIONS

1. What are the key issues that a multimedia designer needs to take into account while integrating text within a multimedia applications.

2.   What are the key issues that a multimedia designer needs to take into acount while integrating sound within a multimedia applications.

3.   What are the key issues that a multimedia designer needs to take into account while integrating video within multimedia applications.

4.   In general what are the three groups that graphic files could be categorized in?

5.   What is MIDI and how does it differ from digitised audio?

6.   Which one of the following video formats would take less storage space: AVI, QuickTime or MPEG?

# 6

# Multimedia Authoring Tools

## 6.1    INTRODUCTION

Having discussed media integration issues as well as multimedia hardware and software, it is clear that creating an interactive multimedia system is more than just creating programming codes. The emphasis in these types of software development is on design, integration, synchronisation and more importantly interactivity. Multimedia authoring tools provide the environment and the framework that multimedia designers require to organises and edit the various elements of multimedia projects including, video, sound, animation, graphics and text. Multimedia authoring tools could be viewed as the glue that binds media elements to the interactivity that is created by the designer.

Authoring tools are like programming languages that enable the integration of text, audio, video and animation into an interactive presentation.

McGloughlin (2001) defines multimedia authoring tools as: computer applications that allow the user to develop a piece of software by dragging and dropping various media components without the need to know, use or understood a programming language. Of course some of the currently available authoring tools like Macromedia Director come with a fully blown programming environment available to the more advance users.

Vaughan (1998) divides multimedia-authoring tools into three general categories. These are:

- Card – or page-based tools
- Icon-based tools
- Time-based tools

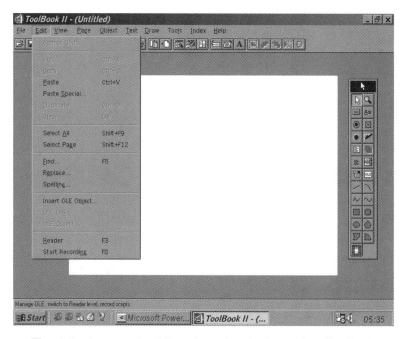

**Fig. 6.1**   An example of Page-based authoring tools – ToolBook

### Card or Page Based Tools

The working metaphor in these authoring tools is based on a book or a page. Working with these authoring tools the designer would create an interactive book. This means that the way the elements are organized are similar to pages of a book or a card file.

The authoring system lets the multimedia designer link these pages or cards into an organized sequence. Good examples of these types of authoring tools are HyperCard and ToolBook. HyperCard is the oldest hypertext-authoring tool launched by Apple in 1987.

We will review ToolBook and its working environment later on in this chapter (Figure 6.1).

### Icon-based Tools

These authoring tools use a flow chart concept to create a map of how various multimedia elements are connected together as well as various characteristics of each individual element. The program typically displays flow diagram of activities along branching paths. A good example of icon-based authoring tools is the Macromedia Authorware. Authorware in one of the leading tools in design and development of learning and training packages (Figure 6.2).

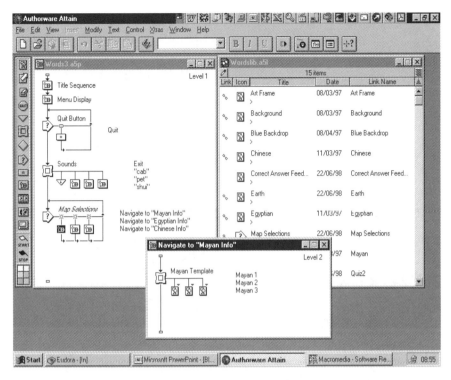

**Fig. 6.2**  An Example of Icon-based authoring tools: Authorware

### Time-based Tools

These authoring systems that view the development of a multimedia package as organising objects along a time line. Sequentially organised frames are then played back to the user. Macromedia Director is a good example of time-based authoring tools (Figure 6.3).

There are also the more traditional type tools that have been upgraded to be able to deal with multimedia production. The most notable of these are Microsoft's range of products including Visual Basic and Visual C++.

Visual Basic is essentially from the family of BASIC (Beginners All-Purpose Symbolic Instruction Code) programming language, one of the first to be developed. According to Microsoft's documentation: Visual Basic has evolved from the original BASIC language and now contains several hundred statements, functions, and keywords, many of which relate directly to the Windows GUI. Beginners can create useful applications by learning just a few of the keywords (Figure 6.4).

Beside the above mentioned authoring tools there are more and more new tools that are emerging almost on daily basis. Some of these are listed below:

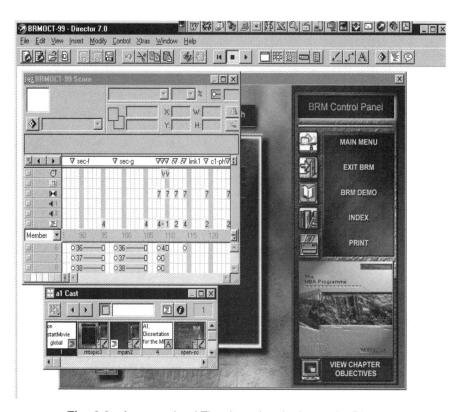

**Fig. 6.3**   An example of Time-based authoring tools: Director

- **Digital Chisel** for Power Macintosh, this package could be used to create presentations, storybooks, lessons, reports, or interactive (more information can be found at: www.digitalchisel.com)
- **HyperSense** comes with a collection of easy-to-use yet powerful tools, which enables designers to produce a wide range of interactive multi-media 'documents' from courseware to complete applications (more information can be found at: www.thoughtful.com).
- **HyperStudio** A 'Constructivist' type of tool which adopts a minimalist design, it is aimed at people and mainly students with no multimedia authoring background (more information can be found at: www.hyperstudio.com).
- **IconAuthor** Another simple interface and relatively restrictive authoring tool that may be of some use if you are starting, but not for advanced authoring. The features provided by the IconAuthor include dialog boxes, list boxes, combo-boxes, and pull-down menus. IconAuthor even provides an interface to allow you to access databases over the Internet (more information can be found at: www.aimtech.com).
- **mTropolis** a powerful authoring tool that comes with a graphic development

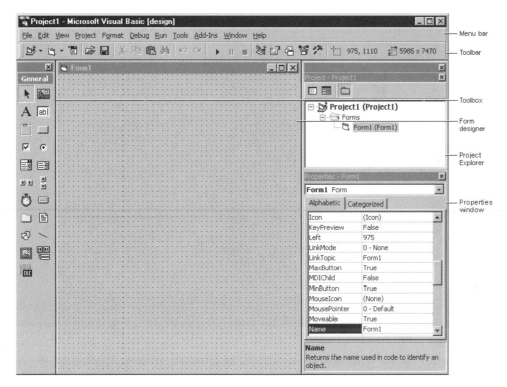

**Fig. 6.4**  Visual Basic working environment (from Microsoft On-line Library http://msdn.microsoft.com/library/

environment creating cross-platform products using object-oriented programming (more information can be found at: www.mfactory.com).

- **Oracle Media Objects** is a tool similar in metaphor to HyperCard, but hooks with Oracles future plans of distributing multimedia via CD-ROM and networks (more information can be found at: www.oracle.com).

## 6.2    WORKING WITH PAGE-BASED TOOLS: TOOLBOOK

Working with ToolBook is like writing a book. The metaphor used in ToolBook is the development of a Multimedia book that could contain various types of objects like:

- Text objects
- Sound objects
- Graphic objects
- Video & Animation objects

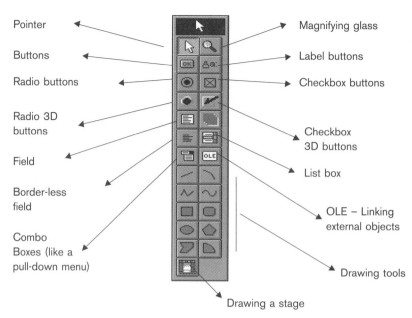

Pointer

Buttons

Radio buttons

Radio 3D
buttons

Field

Border-less
field

Combo
Boxes (like a
pull-down menu)

Magnifying glass

Label buttons

Checkbox buttons

Checkbox
3D buttons

List box

OLE – Linking
external objects

Drawing tools

Drawing a stage

**Fig. 6.5** ToolBooks Tool Palate

ToolBook provides two different working environments: **Authoring Environment** where you author your book and **Reader Environment** where the system shows you what your book looks when it's been read, i.e. its complied version.

Like graphic tools we reviewed earlier on, ToolBook comes with a tool palate that offers multimedia designer various options (Figure 6.5).

Objects form the building blook of application development in ToolBook. Objects are items that you add to your interface to create interactivity or visual effects. A picture on a page, or a text field that the user could edit or a button that the user presses is an object. An important feature of an object is the properties you could associate with it. The properties of an object are sets of instructions that sets various attributes for that object (Figure 6.6).

ToolBook also comes with a 'Property Editor' that allows the direct manipulation of an object's property. This is located in the 'Tools Menu'. There are two different ways in creating a ToolBook application. One is to use an automatic *Book Specialist Template* which is an automatically loaded when ToolBook is first opened or start the project manually. Table 6.1 shows a simple example.

ToolBook can offer full text or Keyword search facility to the users with the built-in search. The first step is to create an index of text. From the menu select the 'Index' option and then decide what Toolbook should be indexing. Once an index file has been created the 'Reading' book options could be set so that when the file is

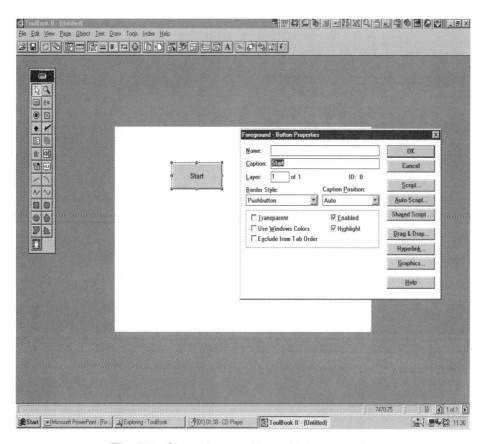

**Fig. 6.6** Shows button object with its properties

executed the reader has a full text search option. To do this from the 'index' menu select 'reader level settings' (Figure 6.7).

ToolBook was one of the first multimedia authoring tools to emerge. Although ToolBook does offer some interesting functionalities to the user including a built-in search engine, but it is very limiting in terms of offering multimedia authors full freedom to develop a complex system. ToolBook is a useful tool for developing training or learning packages.

## 6.3 WORKING WITH ICON-BASED TOOLS: AUTHORWARE

According to Macromedia Authorware is a visual rich-media authoring tool for creating web and online learning. Authorware can:

First let's decide on a background page design for the application. The designer could use different backgrounds for different pages. From the 'Object' menu select background properties. When the background property windows open you could use the 'select resource' button to import graphics into your background

Using the tool pallet you could create a text field to enter a welcome message for the user.

Once you have entered the text you could change its properties like colour, size and style.

ToolBook has a pre-define facility to create 'hyperlinks' between various pages of your book. The 'hyperlink' windows gives the designer options like: Link to next page; Link to previous page; Link to last and first pages; Link to a specific page; Link to a URL address.

Once the designer has finished with a page then other pages can be created. The option for a new page could be found in the 'Object' menu.

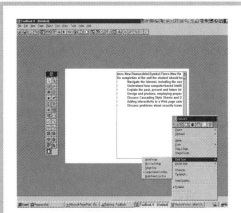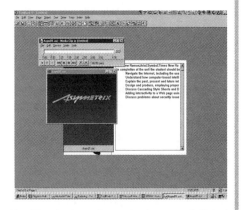

You can use any word processing package like Word to create your text content and then import it into your tool book application. Simply

- Create your text in Word
- Select and Copy text
- Paste it into a text field in ToolBook.

Once you have pasted in your text object then you can change its characteristics like Font, Colour etc.

ToolBook also allows the import of digital video files into your Multimedia book. There are two different ways of importing Video into your Multimedia book

Option 1:  As a generic 'Media Clip'
Option 2:  As a 'Video Clip'

**Table 6.1**  An example of creating an interactive book using ToolBook

- Create interactive, rich-media learning applications
- Deliver learning tools on the web, LANs, and CD-ROM
- Track student progress and results within the learning environment.

Authorware authoring environment consist of five key components: tool bar, icon palette, design window, presentation window and knowledge objects.

Knowledge Objects are one of the key features in Authorware. Knowledge objects are incorporated into an application by dragging them from the Knowledge Objects, window. Some Knowledge Objects are automatically added to your file by other Knowledge Objects or by the New File dialog box. You can edit each Knowledge Object's properties with its wizard. Knowledge objects could be compared to function libraries in traditional languages like C.

As well as a set of default knowledge objects that that come with the standard package one could obtain additional knowledge objects from other developers. (Figure 6.8).

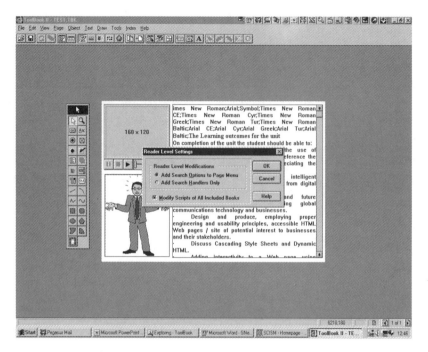

**Fig. 6.7**   Setting the search engine options

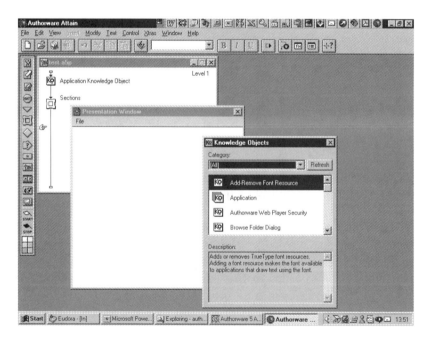

**Fig. 6.8**   Authorware's working environment

The default knowledge objects are organized into the following categories:

- New File
- File
- Internet
- Interface Components

The Application and Quiz Knowledge Objects are available when Authorware starts.

**Application Knowledge Object:** The Application Knowledge Object provides navigation for sections, pages, and quizzes. Select from a variety of layout, delivery, user interface, and other options. The designer can customize this template with his or her own content for a particular discipline or instructional strategy.

**Quiz Knowledge Object:** The Quiz Knowledge Object is a basic testing shell that sets global parameters for the following types of exercises: multiple choice and standard question types. The user can select all the answers that apply to the question.

**File Knowledge Object:** includes the following options:

- **Find CD:** locates the CD-ROM drive on the computer.
- **Set File Attribute:** sets the system attributes (such as Read-only) of external files.
- **Jump to Authorware File:** jumps to other Authorware files from the current piece.
- **Add/Remove Font:** Resource loads a font file into memory so that Authorware can draw text using the font.
- **Copy Files:** copies one or more files into a directory.

**Internet Knowledge Object:** Authorware web player security sets trusting and non-trusting options for Authorware web player. Send E-mail sends a standard e-mail message.

**Interface Knowledge Object:** The Interface KO provides the following functionalities to an application:

- Radio Buttons displays a set of radio-button selection controls.
- Checkboxes displays a set of checkbox selection.
- Slider displays a horizontal or vertical slider control.
- Message box displays a windows-style message or alert box.
- Move Cursor changes the location of the mouse pointer.
- Set Window Caption changes the text in the Presentation window title bar.
- List box displays a Windows-style highlighted list box control in your piece.
- Browse Folder Dialog Box displays a Windows-style dialog box for browsing and selecting directories.

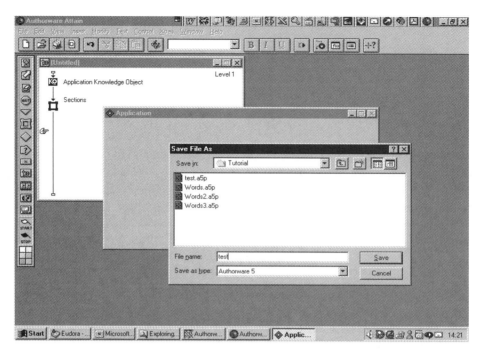

**Fig. 6.9**    Starting the Application Knowledge Object

- Movie Controller displays standard play, pause, stop, rewind, and fast-forward controls for video and audio files.

So let's look at an example.

Selecting an 'Application' knowledge object starts the Wizard, which will help you through creating an 'Application' Figure 6.9.

Once the Application Knowledge Object is activated the user is required to determine a number of options including:

**Delivery Options:** which deals with your details of the product being developed, including the output screen size.

**Application Layout:** : which allows the user to select from a number of pre-defined templates including: 'corporate', 'consumer' and 'education' to create the application.

**Interface Options:** which allows the user to setup various functionality including adding navigation, menu options, etc.

**Content Setup:** which allows the users to add new content text objects to their applications (Figure 6.10).

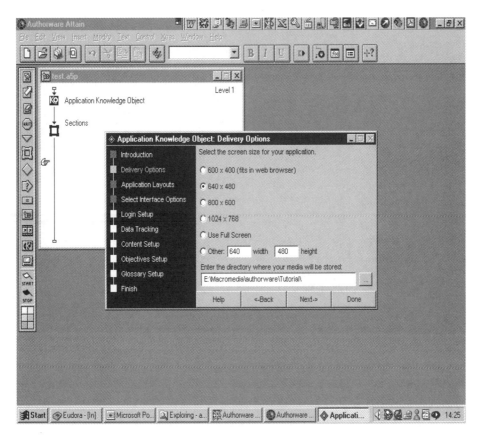

**Fig. 6.10** Setting the delivery options

Once the user has gone through all the options, then Authorware creates a template which includes a menu, navigational structure as well as containers for the content. These could be edited by the designer to create a fully functional application. This is an excellent feature for the novice user as it quickly creates a working prototype that could easily be expanded (Figure 6.11).

Authorware allows you to use a variety of external files within your presentation, including graphic files, digital audio and movies as well as Flash movies as external objects. This can be achieved either by using the importing *file* option or *inserting media element* option available through the insert menu.

Authorware (latest version 6) is a very useful tool in terms of creating quick training and learning tools. The built-in Knowledge Objects that allows quick creation of an application as well as building functionalities such as setting up quizzes, search and bookmaking facilities makes Authorware an ideal tool for developing education type of applications.

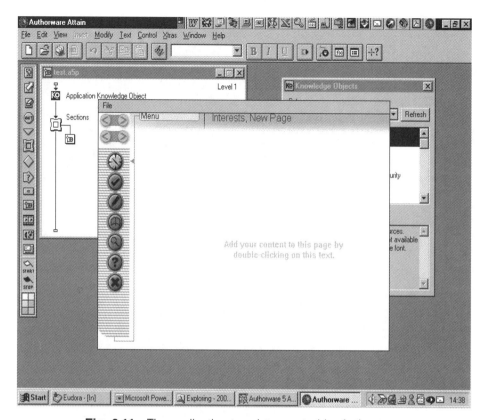

**Fig. 6.11** The application template created by Authorware

## 6.4 WORKING WITH TIME-BASED TOOLS: DIRECTOR

Macromedia's Director is a very powerful and professional multimedia development tool, which comes with a full-blown programming environment called LINGO. The Conceptual framework for Director is making a 'Movie' (Figure 6.12).

Key elements within a 'Movie' are the '*Casts*' that appear on the 'Stage' either sequentially or non-sequentially and 'play' their 'parts' for a given period of 'time'. The '*Score Sheet*' which contains the script of what the 'Casts' should be doing and the '*Stage*' where the movie is played out.

Cast members are the basic building blocks of a Director movie and they could include: shapes, buttons, text, field, lingo script, bitmap, sound, video, animation or other Director movies. Another interesting feature of Director is the creation of 'Sprites'.

Sprites are objects representing when, where and how cast members appear in the movie. By creating multiple sprites, the designer can make a single

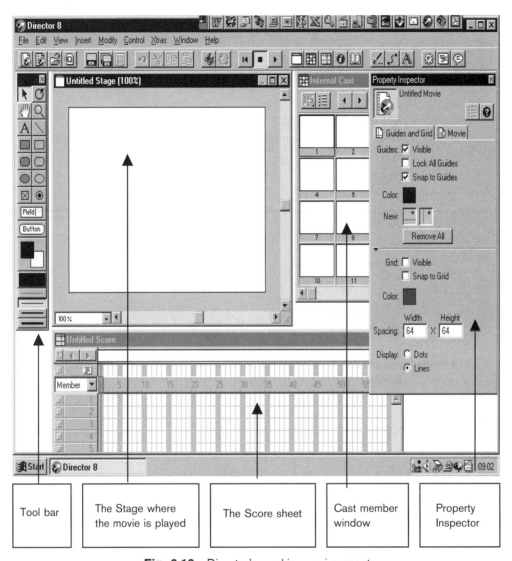

**Fig. 6.12** Director's working environment

cast member appear in different places and different times in a movie. Sprites are created automatically by dragging a cast member to the 'Stage' or 'Score'.

Director's 'score sheet' or window is where the designer creates the script for the movie. The score displays the state of all the elements in the movie over a time period. When a cast is dragged into the stage and hence a sprite is created Director automatically puts the information into the score.

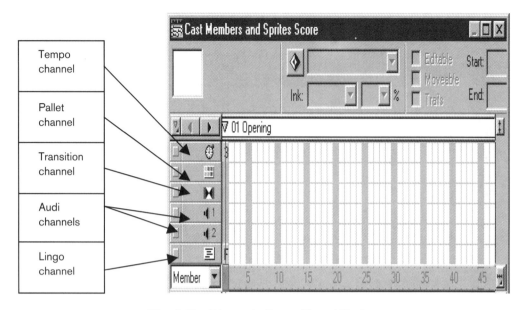

**Fig. 6.13**   Director's Score Sheet Window

The score window also contains other important information, including The speed (tempo) by which the movie is played, the transition effects that could be set for each frame, the audio channel as well as Lingo which could associated with each frame (Figure 6.13).

Lingo is Director's programming and scripting language similar to a natural language structure. Director comes with building Lingo directory and help which is very useful to the novice user. Here is an example of Lingo which when the user clicks the mouse, firstly checks to see if filed cast member number 9 has any input (i.e. any entry) and if not it displays value in this cast member 'Enter Bid' and then plays sound file called 'Thunder' in sound channel number 1.

```
on mouseUp
      if the name of member 9 = EMPTY then exit
      set the hilite of member 'Enter Bid' to TRUE
      sound playFile 1, 'Thunder'
end
```

Let's create a simple example using Director. The first step is to use the file menu and create a new movie. Movie properties, including their output window size, their background and other settings could be fine-tuned using the property inspector. Table 6.2 shows the various stages of creating simple interactive application using pre-prepared graphics.

Director also comes with a large library of pre-defined behaviours that could be assigned to a specific object or cast member. Different types of functionalities including moving forward within a movie, creating rollover effects to more complex tasks such as linking to external Web site can be implemented using Director's behaviour library.

Director files could also be compressed for play-back over the WWW. Director offers the designer the possibility of creating the application in director environment and then save it as a 'Shockwave Movie' which could be played in browsers with shockwave plug-in. Director is one of the best multimedia development tools around and the case studies presented in Chapter 9 were all created using Director.

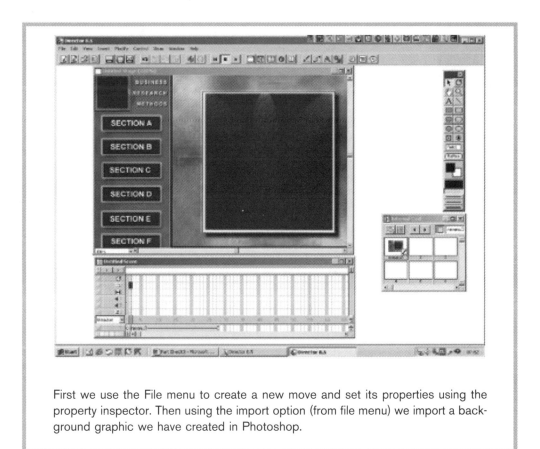

First we use the File menu to create a new move and set its properties using the property inspector. Then using the import option (from file menu) we import a background graphic we have created in Photoshop.

**Table 6.2**  Various stages of creating simple interactive application

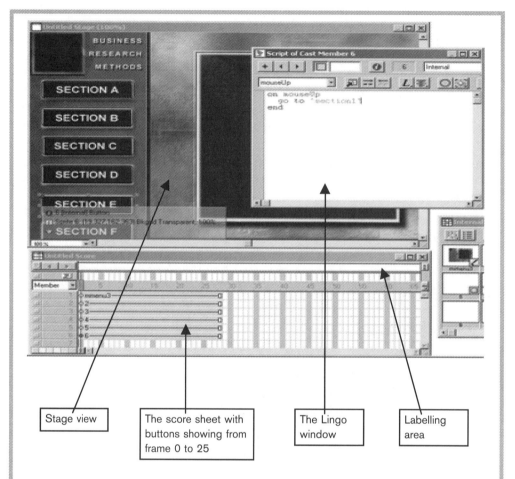

| Stage view | The score sheet with buttons showing from frame 0 to 25 | The Lingo window | Labelling area |

1. Using the tool pallet we create a number of buttons which are then placed on top of the graphic (i.e. over section A, etc.) Using the property inspector we can set the background transparent property to these buttons so that they are visible. By creating these buttons we could then associated various activities with these buttons, including jumping to different parts of the movie. Clicking the Lingo icon associated with each cast member on the cast member windows we could write scripts that add functionality to a specific cast member. In this example once the scripting window is opened we type:

```
On mouseUp
go to 'section 1'
end
```

*which tells the Director to jump to a pre-defined ladled of the movie called section 1.*

**Table 6.2** *continued*

# Chapter Summary

- Authoring tools are like programming languages that enable the integration of text, audio, video and animation into an interactive presentation.
- Multimedia-authoring tools fall into three general categories. These are:
  - Card or page-based tools
  - Icon-based tools
  - Time-based tools
- Working with page based tools is like writing a multimedia book that could contain various types of multimedia objects such as audio and video.
- Working with time based tools is like creating a movie or piece of multimedia presentation that the user interacts with.

# Exercises and Projects

## PROJECT

- Your company wants to develop multimedia in house training. You are asked to research and produce a report of various multimedia authoring tools that are available on the market. Your report should highlight the strength and weakness of each tool with a clear recommendations as to which tool is more suitable for the development of in house training packages.

## RECALL QUESTIONS

1. What is meant by knowledge objects in Macromedia Authorware?
2. What is the difference between cast member and sprite within Director's authoring environment and what is Lingo used for?
3. What is a Shockwave movie and how is it created?
4. What is the key difference between authoring tools such as Director and Authorward and a programming language like C or C++?
5. What are the functions of TEMPO and Transition channels within Director's authoring environment?

# Part III

# Design, Development and Evaluation of Interactive Multimedia Systems

## Human Computer Interaction & IMS, Software Design Methodologies

*This section looks at the broad issue of human computer interaction. Various software design approaches are reviewed in order to give the readers basic understanding of software engineering approach and more importantly how these principles could be used in the design and development of Interactive Multimedia Systems. While Chapter4 and 5 of this section cover the principles of HCI and software engineering issues, Chapter 6 discusses specific models and case studies directly related to the design and development of Interactive Multimedia Systems. Four different case studies are presented taking the reader through various stages of design, development and mplementation.*

# 7

# Human Computer Interaction

*'Human computer interaction is about devices that seem to exhibit a kind of magic. These devices respond with complex contingencies to actions visited upon them by people. They are used to build 'user illusions' of reactive paper or virtual worlds or artificial personae It is concern with the joint performance of tasks by humans and machines; the structure of human-machine communication; the social and organisational interactions with machine design ...'. Card (1993)*

This chapter presents the issues related to Human Computer Interaction (HCI). An overview of the background, concepts, and approaches in interface design and their importance in implementation of interactive multimedia information systems are presented. In addition a brief history of the development of user interface, general guidelines for 'usable' interface and issues related are reviewed.

## 7.1    INTRODUCTION

Various aspects of human computer interaction and relations between computers and their users have been discussed since the creation of computers. But it was in the 1950s and, more specifically, in the 1960s that researchers began to view computers as facilitators of aspects of human creativity and problem solving and therefore the need to define and structure this human computer interaction became apparent. Licklider (1960) was one of the first to propose the term 'man-computer symbiosis' and stated that:

*'The hope is that, in not too many years, human brain and computing machines will be coupled together very tightly and that the resulting partnership will think as no human*

*brain has ever thought and process data in a way not approached by the information machines we know today.'*

This general and vague definition was subsequently clarified and evolved into a science in its own right. According to Card (1993) the emergence of HCI as a professional community dates back to 1982 when the Gaithersburg conference on 'Human Factors in Computing' was held. During the 1980s, as a result of rapid developments in personal computers and software tools, HCI grew enormously as a field of research and gained prominence in the design and development of sophisticated computer applications. Dix *et al.* (1998) pointed out that, as computer use became more widespread, researchers have been concerning themselves with the physical, psychological and theoretical aspects of this process.

It is clearly not the objective of this book to deal with all the various aspects of HCI that now span the fields of science from psychology to cognition and learning. But as Dix *et al.* (1998) pointed out, HCI provides crucial input for those involved in designing learning packages and is an essential part of the design process. Therefore it is necessary to briefly discuss HCI and its main issues and concerns in order to develop an understanding on how design decisions are made during the development of the interactive multimedia systems.

## 7.2    USER INTERFACE, HUMAN FACTORS AND USABILITY

Looking at the HCI extant literature one could not help noticing that a large number of issues regarding the design and implementation of computer packages are grouped perhaps inaccurately under the term of 'user interface'. Johnson (1992) noted that in general 'user interface' is defined as the interface between the user and the computer and could involve both hardware and software. Lewis and Rieman (1993) offer a more comprehensive definition and state that the basic user interface should include items like menus, windows, the keyboard, the mouse, the beep and other computer sounds. This understanding of user interface also includes all the information channels that allow the user and the computer to communicate.

However, the user interaction with computers is influenced by more than just the physical, visible and touchable input and output devices. A typical user of a computer system is often required to understand the meaning and the effects of commands that will allow certain tasks to be achieved. It is the design and presentation of these commands and levels of 'user friendliness' achieved within systems that have formed the corner stone of HCI design discussions. It must be noted that there are differing views on the use and definition of the term 'user friendliness'. Some researchers have criticised the use of the term 'user friendliness' as inadequate and perhaps misleading in defining complex processes such as behaviour of systems and human needs (see Shackel, 1990; Nielsen, 1993). And some have proposed that a more general term such as 'usability' should be applied in evaluating and measuring these processes.

Nielsen (1993) noted that 'usability' applies to all aspects of a system with which a human might interact, including installation and maintenance procedures. According to Shackel (1990) the first attempt to define 'usability' was made by Miller (1971) in terms of 'ease of use', but the concept and a formal definition of usability was given a decade later.

Shackel (1990) defines 'usability' in terms of effectiveness, learnability, flexibility and attitude. Nielsen (1993) expands the definition and proposes the following five 'usability' attributes:

- **Learnability:** The systems should be easy to use, so that the user could immediately be able to work with it.
- **Efficiency:** The system should be efficient to use, so once the user has learned the system, a high level of productivity can be achieved.
- **Memorability:** The system should be easy to remember, so that a casual user is able to return to the system following a period of non-usage, and use it again with no difficulty.
- **Errors:** The system should have low error rate.
- **Satisfaction:** The system should be pleasant to use so that users are subjectively satisfied when using it.

Although 'usability' criteria and guidelines have been widely quoted in the HCI literature (see among others Miller, 1971; Bennett, 1979; Shackel, 1990; Baecker and Buxton, 1990; Preece, 1993; Nielsen, 1993) the practical usage of these guidelines by system developers are still limited. It is also important to note that while a designer could ignore 'usability' guidelines and follow a 'common sense' approach in developing packages, lack of proper attention to the above guidelines could lead to the design of systems that are really not usable. Nielsen (1995) quite correctly points out that:

> *'we have nothing but scorn for any programmer who has the attitude that if users have problems with his or her program then it must be users' fault'.*

Therefore it is clear that a good design approach towards the development of software packages requires the system developer to follow a process which would lead to a system that could satisfy all or some of the 'usability' issues discussed above.

## 7.3    THE DEVELOPMENT OF USER INTERFACE DESIGN

The HCI literature points out that the development of user interface with computer is directly linked to the development of computer technology. Nielsen (1993) observed that user interface technology has been through a series of generations that roughly parallel the generations of computer hardware. These are:

- **Batch systems:** This was the first generation, which is referred to as *zero-dimensional* interface. Here the interaction between a system and a user is restricted to when the batch process is submitted to the system. Batch processing was present in DOS and some versions of Windows operating systems.

- **Line-oriented interface:** This is referred to as *one-dimensional* interface, where the user could interact with a computer on a single line that acts as the *command* line. Once a user concludes the input by hitting the return/enter key, the input cannot be modified and users are not allowed to move about the screen. Line-oriented interface is still present in a typical UNIX operating system.

- **Full-screen interface:** Full screen interface enlarged the space of the interface as well as offering users higher levels of inter-activity compared to line-oriented interface. As a result menu-based systems emerged.

- **Graphical user interface (GUI):** Nielsen (1993) called the 'window interface' a successor to full-screen interface. According to him, the possibilities of overlapping windows added a third dimension to the user interface design and allowed greater degree of inter-activity and flexibility. He also noted that most interface specialists assume that GUIs in general have better usability characteristics than character-based interfaces, especially with respect to learnability for novice users.

- **Next generation interface:** Object Oriented Systems (OOS) are seen as the next generation of user interface. Where the system is divided-up into many different objects that could contain sub-objects of different types that could in turn contain different data types.

The historical development of user interface described above clearly shows that each generation appears to contain some of the features of the preceding generations.

## 7.4   THE DESIGN PROCESS

Software engineering provides the means of understanding the structure of the design process. One of the most widely used approach by Software engineers in going through a design process is the use of a 'life cycle model' in order to identify the activities that occur in a software development process. A classic 'software life cycle' like the 'waterfall' model is presented in Figure 7.1.

As can be seen from the figure above, the graphical representation is reminiscent of a 'waterfall' in which each activity naturally leads into the next. These activities can be briefly described as follows:

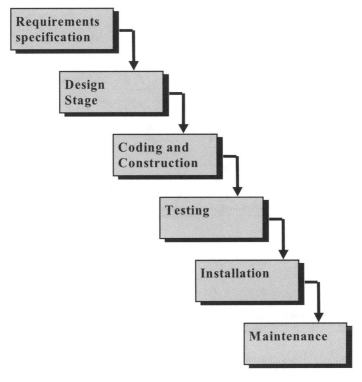

**Fig. 7.1**   The activities in the Waterfall Model of the Software Life Cycle (adapted from Dix *et al.*, 1998)

- **Specifying the requirements:** Where the designer and the client try to work out a description of **what** the eventual system will be expected to provide. This is the first stage in the software product development and the customer is generally outlines the requirements which are discussed with the designer and formulated for system implementation.
- **Design Stage**
  - Architectural design: At this stage the designer determines **how** the system will provide the services expected from it.
  - Detailed design: A detailed description of the systems is provided at this stage, the project is decomposed into manageable components so that it can be implemented in some programming languages.
- **Coding and Construction:** System implementation takes place using a programming language, testing for possible errors follow this.
- **Installation, operation and maintenance:** Once the system has been implemented, it is integrated as described in the architectural design and maintained.

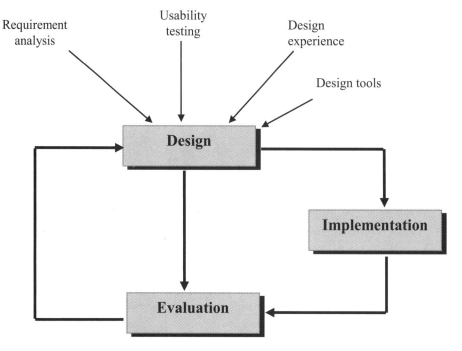

**Fig. 7.2**   User Interface Design Cycle (adapted from Preece, 1993)

The design process as far as the designer is concerned is all about making a series of decisions that focuses the design processes in trying to meet the project requirements. Design procedures and rationale, in their many forms, are therefore aimed at allowing the designers to manage the information about the decision making process and how and why the design decisions were made.

Preece (1993), using the same general principles as the 'life cycle', discusses the user interface design cycle. According to him (see Figure 7.2) there are three suggested main stages in the user interface design. These are: *design, implementation* and *evaluation.*

- **Design stage:** This stage is dominated by collecting information about users' needs and capabilities. *Requirement analysis* (i.e. information gathered about current practices as well as specifying the requirements of the system), *and task analysis* (i.e. details of users' tasks and information about the tasks environment) are carried out and various aspects of interface characteristics and features, including screen design features, metaphors etc. are determined.
- **Implementation/prototyping stage:** Where a prototype system is implemented based on the information gathered.

- **Evaluation stage:** Evaluates the prototype, through feedback from users before the final system is developed.

As far as the designer of IMS is concerned the above principles and discussions form some of the basis on which a robust design and development process could be based on. Shneiderman (1998), quite correctly notes that designers of interactive systems are required to go beyond the intuitive judgements made when dealing with design problems, emerging theories and models offer a framework that are application independent and could be used by the designers of such systems.

## 7.5    USE OF METAPHORS IN INTERFACE DESIGN

The emergence of graphical user interface, and the multimedia technology, which is the seamless integrating of audio, video, animation, graphic and text under the control of a desktop computer have given prominence to the use of metaphors in the user interface design as far as interactive multimedia systems are concerned. Trying to use analogies from the real world, has created enormous interest in the use of metaphors as a strategy for system design (see amongst others: Hammond and Allinson, 1987; Carroll *et al.*, 1988; Smyth *et al.* 1995). Anderson *et al.* (1994) defines the concept of metaphors as an active interaction between two entities:

- the topic, that is the entity to be explained; and
- the vehicle, the familiar entity used in a novel context in order to get across some important points about the topic.

Lynch (1994) pointed out that after some experience with complex abstract systems, computer users begin to construct a conceptual model or 'user illusion' (Kay, 1990) of the system as they imagined it to be organised. This mental model allows the user to predict the behaviour of the system without having to memorise many abstract, arbitrary rules (Norman, 1988). According to Lynch (1994), the primary goal of interface design is therefore to create and support an appropriate and coherent mental model of the operations and organisation of the computer system. Devlin (1993) also states that the only way for a designer to be able to design a potentially useful information system is to adopt appropriate metaphors. According to him designers' understanding of a certain phenomenon amounts to:

- the construction of a suitable metaphor; and
- the identification of points where the metaphor fails.

Interface metaphors, particularly in a hypermedia environment, facilitate what Norman (1993) calls experimental or reactive cogitation. Here the user gains information about the functionality of the system as he or she interacts with various objects in the interface. The user does not memorise any commands, but rather reacts to a rich

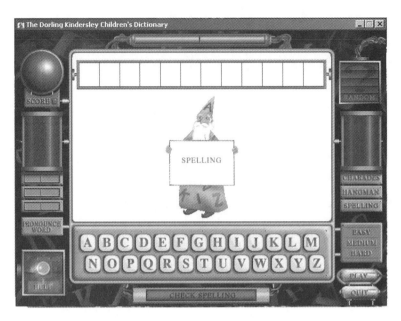

**Fig. 7.3**   Dorling Kindersley's 'Children's Dictionary'

environment of information presented by the interface. Figure 7.3 shows a screen capture from Dorling Kindersley's 'Children's Dictionary' which uses both book and game metaphors to create a rich graphical interface.

It is also important to note that difficulties in the design of graphic interfaces most often arise because of inconsistent or confusing relationships between interface objects and the poor visual design of the computer screen (Lynch, 1994). This problem is exacerbated with the integration of other media such as video and sound into computer systems.

The use of an appropriate metaphor could lead to the successful implementation of a system that should not require the user to learn and remember many rules or procedures. If the user is forced to remember many arbitrary rules then the primary value of the metaphor is lost, because the 'rules' governing users' interaction ought to be self-evident in the metaphor and the interface design.

## Chapter Summary

- Various aspects of human computer interaction and relations between computers and their users have been discussed since the creation of computers. But it was in the 1950s and, more specifically, in the 1960s that researchers began to view computers as facilitators of aspects of human creativity and problem solving, and therefore the need to define and structure this human computer interaction became apparent.

- In general 'user interface' is defined as the interface between the user and the computer and could involve both hardware and software.
- 'Usability' applies to all aspects of a system with which a human might interact, including installation and maintenance procedures.
- The design process as far as the designer is concerned is all about making a series of decisions that focus the design processes in trying to meet the project requirements.

# Exercises and Projects

## PROJECT

Your are required to carry out research into the background and emergence of HCI. Your report should also cover the emergence of 'user interface' and usability and should consider the link between the development of user interface design and the generation of computer hardware over the years. You should also discuss how usability could be used in terms of user interface design.

## RECALL QUESTIONS

1.  What are the usability attributes as defined by Nielsen?
2.  What is the difference between a batch system and line oriented interface?
3.  Discuss what the software life cycle model means and how this could be applied to the process of designing software packages.
4.  What is the difference between user interface design cycle and software life cycle model?
5.  Discuss the importance of use of metaphors in the interface design process.

# 8

# An Overview of Software Design Methods

*'Designing an object to be simple and clear takes at least twice as long as the usual way. It requires concentration at the outset on how clear and simple system would work followed by the steps required to make it come out that way – steps which are more complex than the ordinary ones . . .' Nelson (1977)*

In chapter four the reader was introduced to the basic principles of software and user interface design. Beside the 'software life cycle' model, which has been discussed already, there are other software design and development models that are of significant importance. Although an in-depth treatment of all these models are clearly outside the scope of this book, nevertheless the author believes that an overview of these models will undoubtedly be helpful to the reader. This overview aims to familiarise the reader with approaches and methods that could both be relevant and useful in the design and development of Interactive Multimedia Systems.

Different application development tasks often produce varied design problems and hence require the use of combinations of approaches and models. Among the models briefly covered in this chapter are: Prototyping Model, Rapid Application Development (RAD) Model, Dynamic System Development Method (DSDM), Boehm's Spiral Model, Incremental Model, Component Assembly Model, Concurrent Development Model and Unified Modelling Language (UML).

## 8.1 PROTOTYPING MODEL

The prototyping paradigm, in software development, is based on the premise that the developer builds a partially complete system in order to explore and test some aspects of the system requirements. The prototyping approach is particularly useful as it allows the customer to be involved with the design process and have an input to the design process, hence overcoming some of the potential misunderstandings and ambiguities that could exist in the requirement analysis. Bennett *et al.* (1999) points out that prototyping introduces an iteration approach into the traditional life-cycle model. The HCI literature indicates to the different types of prototyping approach. Dix *et al.* (1998) recognises three main approaches to prototyping. These are:

- Throw-away approach where prototype is built and used for testing aspects of the requirement analysis but the prototype is not kept.
- Incremental approach where the overall system is divided into small increments and the final product is a series of smaller components released as a series.
- Evolutionary prototyping, where in contrast to the throwaway model the prototype is used as the bases for the final product.

Designing a prototype usually starts with requirements gathering and a quick design, then a prototype of the system is produced and given to the customer for evaluation. Once the client is happy with the user interface and indications of functionality offered by the system, then either using the evolutionary approach the prototype is extended to fully incorporate all the requirements or using throw-away method is used to discard the prototype.

Prototyping as a general approach is also quite widely used in developing IMS. It allows direct user interaction with the design process and as an iterative process it allows incremental improvements to be made and hence a much smoother design and development process.

## 8.2   RAPID APPLICATION DEVELOPMENT (RAD) MODEL

Rapid Application Development model is similar to prototyping and rapid prototyping. Indeed, looking at the literature, the difference between RAD and prototyping is not always very clear. While in both approaches the developer aims to build a working model of the system rapidly, the prototyping produces a partially complete system while RAD method aims to produce a fully working system. One of the drawbacks associated with the RAD approach is its requirement for a lot of manpower during development phase.

## 8.3   DYNAMIC SYSTEM DEVELOPMENT METHOD (DSDM)

In 1994 a consortium consisting of a number of larger corporations including IBM, ICL, British Airways, BT, Logica, Data Sciences and many other small organisations was created aimed at producing an industry standard definition of RAD. The DSDM was launched in February 1995. A key principle of DSDM is to build the right system rather than building the system right. According to Stapleton (1998) the DSDM is based on nine underlying principles including:

- Active user involvement in the design and development process;
- DSDM teams are empowered to make decisions;
- The focus of the DSDM is on frequent product delivery;
- The essential criterion for accepting a task is its fitness for business purpose;
- DSDM works on the principle of iterative and incremental developments which allows user's feedback;
- Within a DSDM approach all changes during development are reversible;
- Requirement specifications are agreed at the initial stage at high level of decision making;
- Testing is an integral part of the development life cycle;
- DSDM envisages a collaborative and co-operative approach amongst all interested parties.

Furthermore, using the time boxing approach means that all products of development and prototypes could be re-used for further perfection and there is no opportunity to 'throw-away' any prototypes. Major advantage of this method is that time is considerably saved in the whole development life cycle and software products are delivered rapidly. Amongst the drawbacks listed in the literature are problems associated with getting the right level of support from the users. Similarly if a partner from the team of developers were to pull out, it could create difficulties to replace them with someone of similar ability and knowledge of the project.

## 8.4    BOEHM'S SPIRAL MODEL

The Spiral Model is the combination of the iterative nature of prototyping and the controlled and systematic aspects of the linear sequential model (Pressman, 1997). In this model, software is developed in a series of incremental releases. In earlier iterations a prototype or just a paper model could be developed and in subsequent iteration increasingly more complete versions of the system is released.

Unlike other models that end when the product is released, the spiral model can continue throughout the life of the software. The spiral model maintains the systematic step by step approach used in the classic life cycle, as well as incorporating an iterative framework. As there are no limits to the number of iterations, a better product can be produced since with every new iteration, errors discovered in the earlier iterations can be corrected.

## 8.5    INCREMENTAL MODEL

The Incremental Model also introduces an iterative approach in a typical prototyping environment. An operational product is delivered in each increment. Initial increments may have only contain basic features of the system and as the time progresses, more sophisticated versions are released. An incremental approach normally performs some

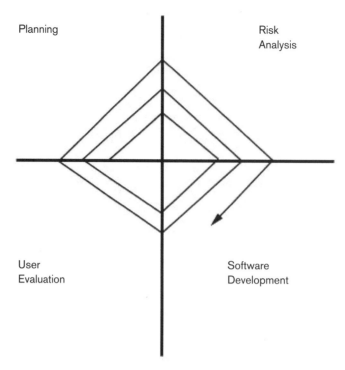

**Fig. 8.1**   Bohehm's Spiral Model (adapted from Boehm, 1988)

initial requirement analysis to identify major tasks that need to be carried out. Another key feature of an incremental model is that it provides the opportunity for the designer to get feedback from users as each increment is developed.

## 8.6   COMPONENT ASSEMBLY MODEL

The Component Assembly Model is also similar to the spiral approach and incremental model and is based on an object-oriented approach. Components or classes are developed in various stages of project development and are stored in a class library for re-use when needed. It is also possible that the first iteration in the application development phase can use existing classes from the library, developing additional classes if necessary. Process flow then follows spiral model and ultimately re-enters the component assembly iteration. A key important significance of this model is its emphasis on software reuse, which could result in cost reductions. However, the use of this model requires the use of object-oriented languages such as C++, Ada, Eiffel, SmallTalk and Java as not every programming language supports object-orientation. Because of the reusability feature of the object-oriented languages Component Assembly Model is also becoming more common.

## 8.7    FORMAL METHODS

Formal Methods use mathematical notation to obtain system's behaviour and function and are therefore considered to be more accurate (Pressman, 1997). The proponents of formal method state that mathematics provides accurate results, which no other tools can provide. Formal methods do not make extensive use of text and diagrams as in non-formal methods therefore they are more precise and less prone to ambiguity.

Opponents perceive formal methods to be rather difficult than graphical and textual methods, and, therefore believe that it should be used mainly in systems where accuracy is of paramount importance, such as, systems, which may have an impact on human lives (i.e. an air traffic control system). Hall (1990), also notes that proponents of formal methods claim that it can revolutionise software development whereas those against it find it too difficult, while a large proportion of the designers and developers are unaware or uninterested in the formal methods.

Mathematics is generally perceived as a rather difficult domain to learn and master. Many analysts/designers do not want complex mathematics in order to capture a system's behaviour because they think they might run into difficulty in achieving their goal easily.

## 8.8    STRUCTURED SYSTEM ANALYSIS & DESIGN METHODOLOGY (SSADM)

Learmonth and Burchett Management Systems (LBMS) and the Central Computing and Telecommunications Agency (CCTA) developed SSADM, as a UK government's standard for systems development and procurement. SSDM has six phases, each with its own sub-tasks. These are:

- Analysis phase;
- Specification Requirement phase;
- User Selection phase;
- Detailed Data Design phase;
- Detailed Procedure Design phase;
- Physical Design Control phase.

Analysis phase aims at creating an overview of the current and ideal data flows and a logical structure. Specification requirement phase involves defining audit control and security and extending logical data structure. Required data flows are created in this phase and process outlines defined. In the user selection phase, users' options are created, assisting users in selection and setting performance objectives. The detailed data design phase involves carrying out third normal form (3NF) data analysis, as well as the creation of detailed logical data structure, building of composite data structure and setting up of data dictionary. In the detailed procedure design phase the physical design control and the design of manual procedures are implemented. In the last phase, the physical design control, system test plan is designed and program specifications are created. Operating schedules and files and database definitions are also created in this phase and user manuals are written. Data Flow Diagrams (DFD's), Entity/Event Matrix and Function/Event Matrix, Entity Life History Diagrams and Normalisation Procedures are used to achieve goals of these activities. The SSADM is not a natural choice for Object-Oriented system development and there are other methodologies that are more suited for object-oriented development (Avison *et al.*, 1994). A common problem associated with the use of SSADM is that this methodology requires too much documentation and duplication (for cross-checking earlier stages) and is very time consuming. Most government projects in Britain used this methodology and according to the literature hardly any product was delivered on time. As SSADM philosophy involves too much time on analysis and design, by the time a product is developed its requirement could well require changes.

## 8.9    OBJECT ORIENTED SYSTEM DESIGN (OOSD)

Object-oriented systems analysis and design models have emerged as one of the key design approaches over the last decades. OOSD views system developments as establishing relationships between objects and actions associated with them. Coad and Yourdon (1990) define an object as:

> *An abstraction of something in a problem domain, reflecting the capabilities of the system to keep information about it and interacts with it or both.*

For example we could look at three objects, mechanic, car, spanner and the action repair. We could then observe that the mechanic, who *performs* the repair *acting upon* the car, *using* the spanner. Object oriented system design encourages code re-use and has characters like encapsulation, inheritance and polymorphism (the ability to appear in many forms). The literature on OOSD contains different OO modelling languages and methods, some of which are briefly covered below.

### 8.9.1    Object Modelling Technique (OMT)

James Rumbaugh and his colleages at General Electric's Shenectady Research and Development Centre (Rumbaugh *et al.*, 1991) developed OMT. This method relies on a 'bottom up' approach and views the design process as being divided up into three main phases including:

- Analysis phase: which models the problem domain;
- Design phase: where the result of the analysis phase are structured and;
- Implementation phase: which takes into account target language constructs.

OMT has three clear stages at analysis phase: object modelling, dynamic modelling and functional modelling. Object Modelling involves identifying classes and their relationships and building class diagrams, which show relationships with one another. Dynamic behaviour of a class is described in Dynamic Modelling using state diagrams and event flow diagrams. Functional Modelling involves identifying operations and putting them together by means of data flow diagrams. OMT then builds on to design phase where all diagrams from the analysis phase are further improved (Brittan *et al.*, 2000). OMT has been very influential in the development of other OOSD methods including UML. For example OMT's class diagram notation is incorporated into UML almost unaltered. Among the advantages of OMT, the literature notes the step-by-step support, which it provides during the analysis phase and the idea of a seamless development process, which it strongly emphasises. On the negative side it is weaker in its guidance during the design and implementation phases where it provides general guidelines and some heuristics.

### 8.9.2   OOSE Objectory

Objectory, like OMT is a key contributor to the development of UML. According to (Brittan *et al.*, 2000), Ivar Jacobson invented OOSE for object-oriented modelling. Objectory method is used for building a number of systems as diverse as a tele-communication system for Ericsson and a financial system for Wall Street. As can be seen from Figure 8.2 Objectory method has three phases: Analysis, construction and testing phase.

The Requirement phase uses a natural language description of what the system should do to build three models (use case model, domain model and user interface descriptions). The Analysis model is a refinement of the domain object model produced in the requirements phase. The construction phase refines the models produced in the Analysis phase.

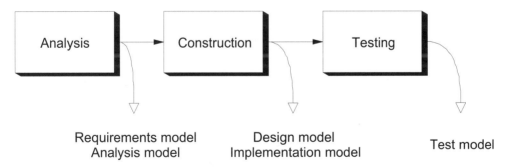

**Fig. 8.2**   Processes and Models in Objectory (adapted from Bennett *et al.*, 1999)

### 8.9.3    Booch Method

Brittan *et al.* (2000) notes that the Booch Method is also known as Object Oriented Design with Attributes (OODA) and provides a step-by-step guide to the design of a system. These steps first identify classes and objects then their semantics and relationship and eventually implement them. During these steps class diagrams and object diagrams are produced and packaged together by module diagrams. OODA views the design process as a highly incremental and iterative process.

### 8.9.4    Fusion

Developed by Hewlett-Packard, Fusion is based on experiences of several initial methods and uses a large number of model diagrams. This method claims to be a 'fusion' of the good concepts of other methods. It has improved ideas and techniques for the specification of operation and interaction between objects. Fusion has three phases: analysis, design and implementation. Each phase has a set of detailed steps and the output of one step acts as the input for the next. This can be considered a plus but on the minus side, it is very complex and requires a sophisticated Computer Aided Software Engineering (CASE) tool without which it is almost impossible to produce a consistent and complete design.

### 8.9.5    Object Oriented Analysis and Design (OOAD)

The OOAD is based on a theoretical foundation, consisting of logic and set theory and attempts to integrate the static and dynamic aspects of OO analysis. In this method object flow diagrams are used to model high-level processes, event schemas are used to describe object behaviour, and object schemas are used for describing static object types and their relationships.

As there were so many methods on offer for object-oriented analysis and design, it could be quite confusing to a novice to the field and even system designers and developers. The authors of many of these models have realised that a common method would be more beneficial in the long run and the cooperation between designers and system analyst have led to the birth of a unified method called Unified Modelling Language (UML).

### 8.10    UNIFIED MODELLING LANGUAGE (UML)

According to Booch, Jacobson and Rumbaugh (the 'three amigos' who invented the UML) UML could be defined as:

> *'The Unified Modelling Language is a third-generation method for specifying, visualizing, and documenting the artifacts of an object-oriented system under*

*development. The Unified Modelling Language represents the unification of the Booch, Objectory, and OMT methods and is their direct and upwardly compatible successor... Our goal is to make the Unified Modelling Language the basis for a common, stable, and expressive object-oriented development method.' (For more details see: http://www.microgold.com/Stages/UML_FAQ.html)*

As stated above Unified Modelling Language (UML) is a modelling language for object-oriented system development, which unifies concepts of many object-modelling languages. UML, since its adaptation by Object Management Group (OMG), the leading organisation for standards within the object-oriented field, in 1997, has become a standard for modelling language. UML consists of three key elements:

- A formal meta model;
- A graphical notation;
- A set of idioms of usage;

In UML, primarily, there are nine different diagrams to capture the static, dynamic and architectural behaviour of the system model. Case diagrams are used to capture requirement of a system. Class and Object diagrams are used to capture static structure of the system. Activity, Sequence, Collaboration and State diagrams are used to capture the dynamic behaviour. Component and Deployment diagrams are used to show physical architecture of the system (Stevens *et al.*, 2000).

In addition there are extensions (tagged values, stereotypes and constraints) as well. The extension mechanism allows the inclusion of new attributes, different semantics and additional constraints. Extensions are also used to model additional features for web application. The literature, however indicates that there is a lot of debate about which modelling language can model the web applications better. Pressman (1997) notes that 'although object-oriented methods appear to have the best combination of features for modelling a client server system, conventional methods (data flow diagram, entity-relationship diagram and structure chart) can also be adopted.'

Although UML is not meant for modelling structured software development, it has an ability to replace some aspects of structured system modelling. For example, UML use case diagrams can explain what their counterpart data flow diagrams do but only better. It seems so natural to think top level view in use cases where 'actors' can be seen as proper role players rather than 'source' or 'sink' in structured system. Similarly 'state transition diagrams' in UML can capture dynamic behaviour of a system more effectively than their structured modelling counterpart 'entity life history' because the former captures every state of every class.

UML can be used in the different phases in the system development life cycle, from the requirement specification to the testing of an end product. It can be used to describe systems without any software too. UML can be used to model information

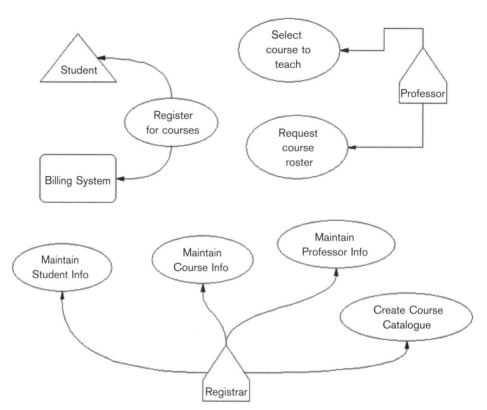

**Fig. 8.3** A Typical UML case diagram depicting a course registration system (*adapted from Quatrani, 1998*)

systems, technical systems, embedded real-time systems, distributed systems, system software, business systems and the list is endless. Forward and reverse engineering is possible with UML. This clearly shows how versatile UML is.

However, developing software systems is an evolutionary process. Systems almost unthinkable a decade ago are now being developed. System design process is also evolving to cater for these systems. Although UML's Extension mechanism is established to cater for new dimensions in modelling world it is still arguable whether it will meet needs of evolving systems. During these evolving situations it would be rather unconvincing to suggest that the current method or rather method of the last century will capture the requirement of a system that may not yet have been born. Client server systems can be taken as an example. Distributed computing has brought about client-server computing to a different height. One particular method is not sufficient for client-server modelling. Pressman (1997) notes that, 'debate continues on the best analysis and design approach for client-server systems.' It is difficult to say that UML fills in this gap either. Some aspect of client-server modelling can be better modelled by using notations from conventional modelling system such as data flow diagram and entity-relationship diagram. UML may have its strength in most situations but it certainly has inadequate features to fully model client server systems.

No tools can be flawless. Because of several diagrams involved, UML is daunting to learn and takes much longer to master. Bjorkander (2000) concludes that despite UML's strength in the early phases of the development process, it does leave some things to be desired in the system design and implementation phases because it is lacking in structural and behavioural constructs. However, it has far less drawbacks than other object-oriented modelling methods.

The discussion in the current chapter clearly indicates that while there are similarities in the different design approaches covered, namely the need to go through key stages such as requirement analysis, dcsign analysis and implementation and testing, there is very little if any guidelines or models to organise the design of the user interface.

Other approaches and models including storyboarding and the IMS design model are discussed in the next chapter which aims to use traditional design and development approaches as well as new models to map out the process of designing, testing and implementing an Interactive Multimedia system.

## Chapter Summary

- Different application development tasks often produce varied design problems and hence require the use of combinations of approaches and models.
- The prototyping paradigm, in software development, is based on the premise that the developer builds a partially complete system in order to explore and test some aspects of the system requirements.
- Formal Methods use mathematical notation to obtain system's behaviour and function and are therefore considered to be more accurate.
- Object-oriented systems analysis and design models have emerged as one of the key design approaches over the last decades. OOSD views system developments as establishing relationships between objects and actions associated with them.
- Unified Modelling Language (UML) is a modelling language for object-oriented system development, which unifies concepts of many object-modelling languages.

# Exercises and Projects

**PROJECT**

Using an appropriate design and development method model the following system.

A typical course registration system where students select courses, register in the course and the information is then processed in order to produce internal records for billing and class allocation.

**RECALL QUESTIONS**

1.   What are the key phases in the 'Fusion' model of design?
2.   What is SSADM and what are the key phases of the SSDM design process?
3.   Discuss what is Boehm's Spiral model and how this model approaches the process of software design and development.
4.   What are the different types of prototyping and how do they differ from each other?
5.   What are the key components of the UML and what are they used for?

# 9

# Design and Development of Interactive Multimedia Systems (IMS) A Case Study Approach

*'Human-computer interaction is about devices that seem to exhibit a kind of magic. These devices respond with complex contingencies to actions visited upon them by people. They are used to build 'user illusions' of reactive paper or virtual worlds or artificial personae It is concern with the joint performance of tasks by humans and machines; the structure of human machine communication; the social and organisational interactions with machine design . . .' Card (1993)*

In Chapters 7 and 8 the principles and various models of software design and development were discussed in order to provided the reader with a general overview of the key issues in what we broadly call human computer interaction. The aim of this chapter is to take a hand on approach exploring the application of theory in practice and to take a closer look at the process of designing and developing interactive multimedia systems.

## 9.1    GETTING STARTED

The reader would have gathered by reading the previous two chapters that there are number of common features in the variety of design and development approaches that were reviewed. Almost all the different design models from the 'life cycle' model to prototyping, and even some of the object oriented design approaches view the process of designing software systems as going through a series of steps (commonly in an iterative manner). These common features and steps are:

- Identifying the requirements of the system;
- Identifying the design issues;
- Implementation;
- Testing and evaluation;

While recognising these general steps are clearly helpful in getting a project started, they are not enough to guide the designer through the complex process of designing and developing interactive multimedia systems. An interactive multimedia system requires detailed and well-planned approach towards media integration issues. Handling mix of various medium such as audio, video, animation, text and graphics present the designer with a challenge in terms of video and audio asset management as well as synchronisation management in design.

Furthermore, as we have discussed already an interactive multimedia system or a hypermedia system requires careful planning in terms of its navigational structure and the approach used in creating interactivity using an appropriate design metaphor. The IMS design and development cycle presented in Figure 9.1 attempts to addresses the issues discussed above.


## 9.2   STAGES OF IMSDD CYCLE

The stages of the IMS design and development cycle could be defined as follows:

- **System Requirements:** this stage is comparable to the 'requirement specification' in the 'waterfall model' (see Chapter 7) and contains elements of 'feasibility' and 'hardware selection' presented in the RMM model (see Chapter 8). At this stage a general definition of the IMS and its environment as well as tools used for its development are determined. This stage has the following key functions:

  1. To provide a system definition, which outlines the aims and objectives of the system;
  2. To clarify whom the potential users of the system are and if there are any specific requirements that needs to be taken into consideration. For example if we are designing a learning package to teach sign language to users that are hard of hearing, using audio as means of presenting information is clearly not appropriate, hence we also need to pay particular attention to types of information we use and the design approach we take in presenting the information.
  3. To critically evaluate the required hardware as well as the available software platforms and authoring tools and make appropriate choices.

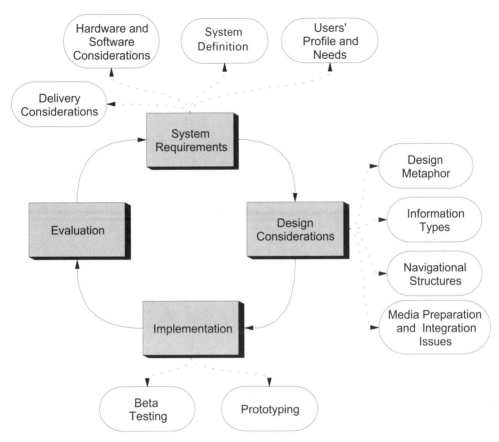

**Fig. 9.1**   Interactive Multimedia System Design & Development Cycle Dastbaz©

4.  To consider carefully the delivery platform required for the system. Clearly developing a distributed interactive multimedia system running on a network environment (either a LAN or WAN) needs a different approach in terms of design and development than a stand alone CD-ROM type of system.

• **Design Considerations:** The purpose of this stage is to draw up clear guidelines about the design details. In this respect this stage could be compared to the 'architectural design' and 'detailed design' stages of the 'waterfall' model and/or the 'design' stage of user interface design cycle proposed by Preece (1993) (see Chapter 7). This stage aims to address the following issues:

1.  *Design Metaphor*: Selecting a 'real world mental model' to be used as the key interface design solution for the system (i.e. a movie, a book, a game, ... etc.)

2. *Information types and formats*: To define the types of information that needs to be integrated into the system, i.e. text, graphics, sound, video and animation. For example an interactive multimedia system about the films and cinema would indicate that video type of content would perhaps be a required on a large scale. While an encyclopaedia system would require a more balanced mix of content with more emphasis on textual type of information.

3. *Navigational structures*: To articulate a clear navigational strategy, including the link structure and features that would avoid cited problems associated with hypermedia systems such as 'disorientation'.

4. *System controls*: To clarify the types and features of controls and tools needed for the systems. These could include retrieval tools, sound, video and animation controls, book marking facilities, etc.

- **Implementation:** Once the design features are defined, the implementation phase of the system begins using multimedia-authoring tools. The implementation stage consists of

(a) Creating a prototype of the system, and

(b) Beta test the prototype for possible design and control problems.

This stage could be compared to the *coding, integration and unit testing* stages in the 'waterfall' model; or the *implementation* stage in the user interface design cycle, the *implementation* stage in OOHDM design model and the *construction* stage in the RMM design model (see Chapters 7 and 8 for more details).

- **Evaluation:** At this stage the system is evaluated against its stated goals. Different types of evaluation approaches including formative or summative could be used (see Chapter 10 for more details).

## 9.3   GUIDELINES FOR INTERFACE DESIGN IN IMS

Shneiderman (1998) discussing theories, principles and design guidelines which could be applied to most interactive systems outlines the 'eight golden rules of interface design' Based on Shneiderman's proposed set of rules and authors' practical experience the following sets of guidelines are proposed for developing the user interface in an IMS.

1. **Use appropriate metaphor:** A good metaphor creates an easy environment that the user could easily recognise and 'feel at home with'.

2. **Simplicity and ease of use is king:** A good interface is one that enables the user to almost immediately start carrying out simple tasks without the need to go through a chunky manual.

3.  **Consistency in design is crucial:** Consistency allows users to develop a feel of the system and is directly linked to both *ease of use* and *memorability* of a system. Consistent use of icons and navigational features helps reduce the complexity of an interface within interactive multimedia systems and hence reduce the cogitative overhead as far as users are concerned.

4.  **The necessity for informative help and feedback:** Provides help tips and feedback to users, in the form of rollover pop-ups (i.e. when the user moves the mouse over an icon) and content sensitive help provides novice users with reliable mechanisms to explore the system and quickly master the ins and outs and key features of the system.

5.  **Provide mechanism for reversal of actions:** A key functionality that needs to be considered by the designer of an IMS is to build-in control features that allow users to correct their mistakes easily and reverse a process they have started inadvertently. A typical approach could be the inclusion of 'history' type bookmarks where the user is given a list of the last actions/commands executed by the system, which could then be reversed.

## 9.4   CASE STUDIES

Having discussed various aspects of design and development of interactive multimedia systems let's now look at four different case studies and examine how our theoretical models and understanding of the design process could apply to the developments of interactive multimedia system.

### 9.4.1   Case Study I

An Interactive Learning Tool (ILT) for 'Learn Quick Institute'

**1. Initial project definition:** '*We have noticed that our first year undergraduate students studying market research are having difficulty grasping the topics covered in the unit and therefore would like to develop a multimedia learning tool that could be used as an additional learning resource . . .*'

It is quite common that the initial project definition is vague and requires further clarification. Holding regular meetings with the client and clarifying key issues as far as system definition and user profiles are concerned, are key activities before the design process starts.

**2. Applying the IMSDD Cycle**

1.  **System Requirements:** The project definition of the system provided by the client gives the initial crucial information upon which we could complete our system requirements. We know that the system is a learning tool, the target

user audiences are students and with further investigation we determine that the client requires the system to run on their PC labs, which is running Windows© NT. This helps us with the process of choosing the appropriate authoring tools to start the development work. Multimedia authoring tools were discussed in Chapter 6 and as we are developing a learning tool an appropriate authoring tool to use would be Macrodemedia's Authorware.

2.   **Design Considerations:** As we are developing a learning tool a number of metaphor options could be considered, including book, classroom and lecture presentation. For the purpose of this project we chose a lecture presentation metaphor where the user could select various lectures and go through them on their own pace. The content provided by the client were some hundred and fifty pages of notes and some power point slide presentations plus video clips on market research, group and in-depth interview techniques. While it is clear that the bulk of the content provided is text based, nevertheless the client requires enhancements to the textual information by inclusion of audio, video and animated examples, which could help the users to better understand the issues presented to them. As far as media preparation and integration issues are concerned there is clearly a need to plan for both digital audio and video production. While the client has provided us with an analogue video tape this needs to be captured and edited digitally before it can be used. The navigational structure of the system is also very crucial. The client ideally requires a system that is simple to use and in terms of navigation can be easily handled by totally novice users. Furthermore, the designer needs to look at the content provided by the client in order to establish how enhancements could be made. In this case study, a sizeable chunk of the text covering 'Scales and Their Measurements' was replaced by animated examples containing audio.

### 3. Visualising the User Interface & Getting Users Feedback

Before starting the implementation of a prototype it is always good practice to try and visualise the user interface and get feedback from the client and potential users. A very powerful method that could be used is the **Storyboard** technique. Used for years in the film industry, a series of drawings are used to provide the director with a visual tool to see how the film's story is developing scene by scene. Storyboarding is a useful technique to visualise the user interface in an IMS, before full system implementation starts. Below are storyboards developed with typical comments from the client.

It is through these sets of iterative exercises and feedback from client/users that the designer of the IMS can refine its user interface and produce a blue print upon which the actual system can be built. From the storyboard a prototype was produced (Figure 9.3).

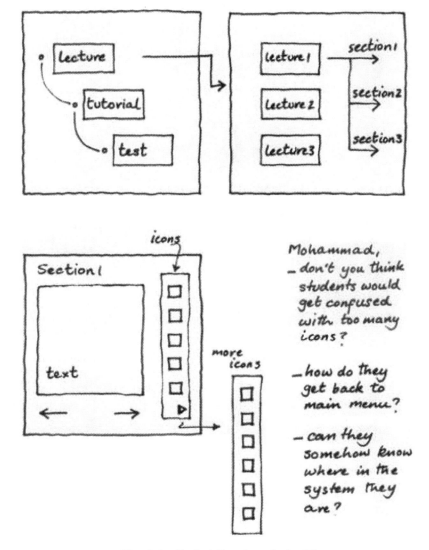

**Fig. 9.2**   Typical Storyboards for ITL

As can be seen from Figure 9.3, modifications have been made to the original storyboard outline, simplifying the interface as well as adding new navigational structures to the system.

As discussed in earlier chapters, navigating through hypermedia systems and the way links are organised is one of the most important aspects of designing IMS systems. A well-cited problem with a number of hypertext and hypermedia systems is that of 'disorientation' or 'getting lost in hyperspace syndrome' which results from poor navigational designs.

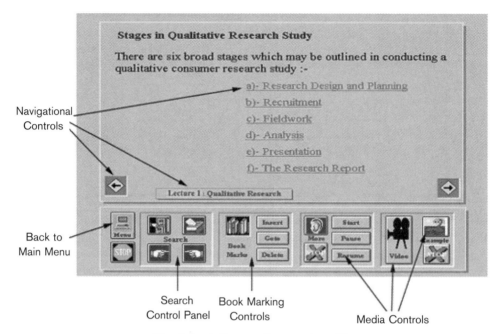

**Fig. 9.3**   A Screen Capture from ITL

As can be seen from Figure 9.4 ITL's link structure has clearly defined routes and return pathways. Once a user follows a link down the end destination the system always provides a rouote back to the start point. An example of the possible paths taken in the ITL structure is as follows:

Lecture 1 ⇔ Page 1.1 ⇔ Page 1.2 ⇔ Page 1.3 ⇔ ... Page 1.n → Lecture 1

The structure could be compared to a closed loop that stops users wandering down routes that have no clear return pathway. Although this could be criticised as limiting users' choice in selecting a path it nevertheless ensures that any path traversed would return to its points of origin thus reducing the possibility of encountering the 'getting lost in hyperspace' syndrome. The problem is better visualised if we look at the complexity of the options that could exist in terms of all the possible path and branches. Figure 9.5 shows the actual flow diagram for just one of the lecture sessions.

**4. Implementation (Prototyping and Beta Testing):** Based on the decisions made during system requirement and design stages a beta version of the ITL was developed. The prototype was tested for possible programming bugs and then critically reviewed by both client and students allowing for further modifications to be made to the prototype.

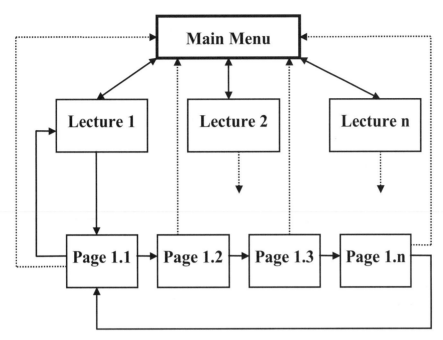

**Fig. 9.4**  Link Structure for ITL

**5. Evaluation:** The evaluation of the ITL system in terms of its design and usability and whether it met its original stated aims and goals was carried out using a summative method (see Chapter 10 for more details).

### 9.4.2    Case Study II

A Multimedia Expert System for 'Hear' A Hearing Aid Manufacturer

**Initial project definition:** *'Hear' is a leading manufacturer of hearing aids in the world. There are two types of products manufactured by the company with distinct features and range of functionalities. We require an interactive system that could act as tool for clinics and patients alike helping them with the process of selecting different types of hearing aids which best meets their clinical as well as aesthetic needs...'*

This is an unusual project since the client primarily requires an expert system with some multimedia enhancements, including audio and animation to show the range of functionalities offered by the products. Therefore, the design process is overshadowed by techniques required in developing a typical expert system. Clearly it is outside the scope of this book to offer an in-depth discussion on expert systems but in order for the reader to have an idea of the issues involved in the design and development of expert systems a brief discussion is offered below.

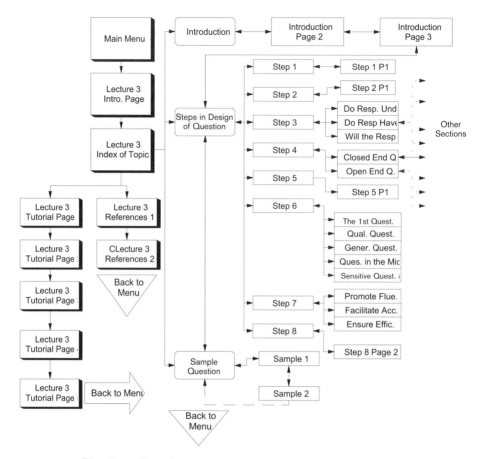

**Fig. 9.5**   Flow diagram for one of the lecture sessions of ITL

An expert system is a computer system that encapsulates specialist knowledge about a particular domain of expertise and is capable of making decisions within that domain (Jackson, 1990). There are different types of expert systems including:

- **Knowledge-Based Systems:** which are intelligent front ends for accessing large databases. Such systems could assist with enquiries.
- **Decision Support Systems:** which are systems to assist users in the decision making process and the interpretation of answers.
- **Consultation Systems:** which are systems that can perform reasoning in order to produce a diagnoses or a report. and
- **Problem Solving Systems:** which are systems capable of reasoning and offering diagnosis and even solutions (for more details see Greenwell, 1988).

A typical expert system consists of knowledge base and an inference engine, which is a computer program that guides the manipulation of knowledge contained in the knowledge base. There are many different ways that the inference engines could reason inferentially and control the reasoning process and manipulation of data. One of the key issues in developing expert systems is the issue of how expert knowledge is represented within the system. A common way knowledge is represented in Knowledge Based Systems is by 'Rules'.

Rule-based systems: depict knowledge using if..then rules. Rule-based systems are often referred to as 'Production Rules'. A typical rule-base system could be:

> IF <condition>
> AND ...
> THEN <action>
> AND <action>

Having briefly discussed what is meant by an expert system let's review the steps required to design and develop such systems. Developing expert systems requires numerous contacts with the client and particularly the experts who will be providing the knowledge to develop the knowledge base. Therefore, an incremental prototyping approach would be a useful technique to use as it allows incremental developments of the systems as well all-round user/client involvement with the design process.

**1. System Requirements:** We know that the system is a multimedia expert system for medical clinics. The aim of the system is to act as an expert consultant in helping clinical staff to provide the best advice to their patients requiring hearing aids. Product technical information as well as knowledge about the decision making process elicited through in-depth interviews with clinical staff forms knowledge base of the system. According to information provided by the client most clinics use PC based systems running Windows™ operating system.

In order to develop an inference engine we need an authoring tool that has extended scripting capabilities and would allow the designer to develop relatively complex range of functionalities for the system. Among the authoring tools reviewed in Chapter 5, Macromedia's Director offers a fully blown programming environment in the shape of **Lingo**, which makes it an ideal candidate for authoring this project.

**2. Design Considerations:** As we are developing a consultative type of an expert system, one of the metaphor options that could be considered is a consultant using a questionnaire to diagnose the problem. Both the clinic staff and patients already use traditional questionnaires and, therefore, the use of a questionnaire metaphor would make the system easier to understand. The client provided information about the types of products they offered. This included video promotions, advertising material, as well as textual technical data about the products. Again as with previous case studies there

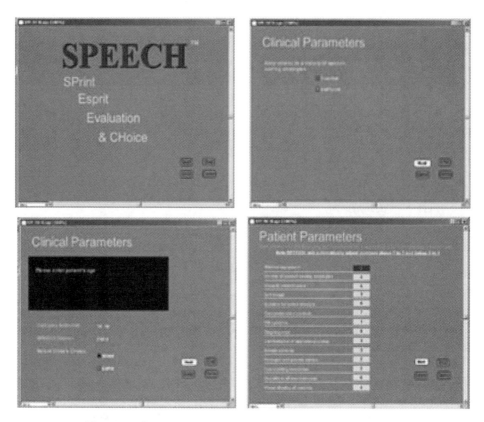

**Fig. 9.6**   Screenshots from the initial prototype developed

is a need for media preparation to create audio recordings as well as transferring the analogue video into a digital format.

**3. Implementation:** An initial prototype system was built and tested with the client and users. The prototype contained eleven data entry screens to gather clinical data, plus a further seven screens acquiring patient's requirements and preferences. It was also crucial to build extensive error trapping functionalities into the package in order to stop users entering erroneous data (Figure 9.6).

The feedback process provided useful information about users' experience and difficulties with the initial prototype. The users observed that it took them some 20 minutes to go through all the eleven screens. They also noted that as the system had extensive error trapping procedures, checking every entry for data integrity, the process was even more taxing. Overall they found the whole process very time-consuming and laborious. Furthermore, they noted that it would be useful if the system could provide them with a summary of the data that had been entered, in

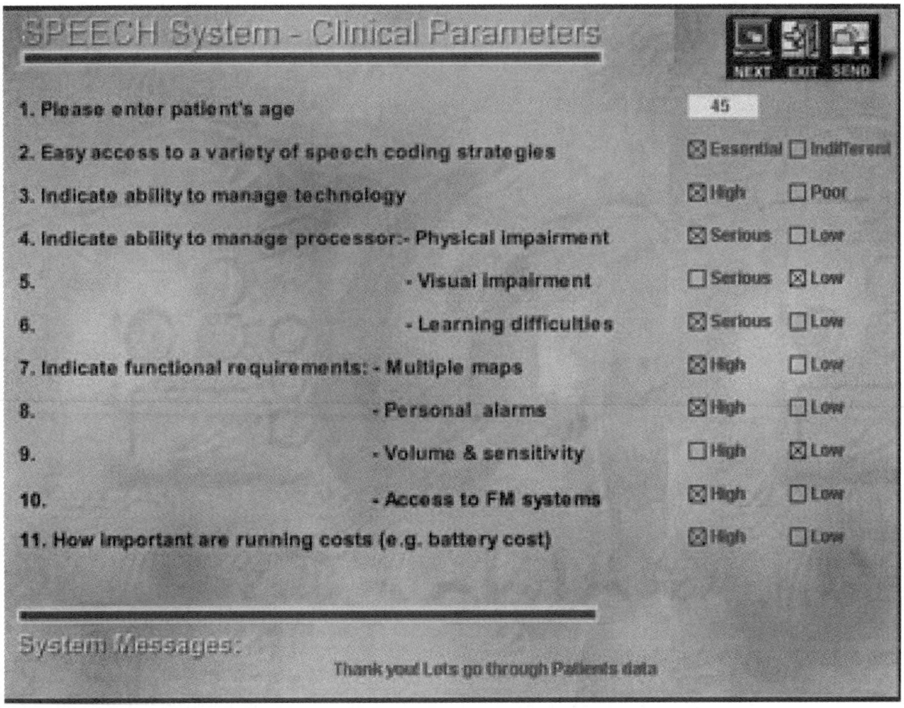

**Fig. 9.7**  Screen captures from 'Speech' showing the 11 data entry screens packed into one screen

order to view how to make the decision making process followed by the package more transparent to the user. Following client feedback extensive changes were made to the interface design and the mechanics of the system (Figure 9.7 and Figure 9.8) in order to overcome the problems noted by the users. The eleven separate screens for data entries were reduced to one and the system provided more summary of the data entered by users.

As stated earlier on, the inference engine for the system was developed using Director's Lingo (Figure 9.9). It took some two thousand lines of code to create both the extensive error trapping routines as well as the inference engine to interrogate the rule-based system. Multimedia enhancements including audio help files and an informative video clip about the products and how the system worked were added. Audio was also used to warn users when data entries were incomplete or values were entered erroneously.

**4. Evaluation:** The 'Speech' system developed was given to a number of clinics for a six months' formative evaluation. The final version of the system had in-built tracking facilities that observed how clinicians used 'Speech' and recorded the process they followed making their decisions. The data gathered from the six

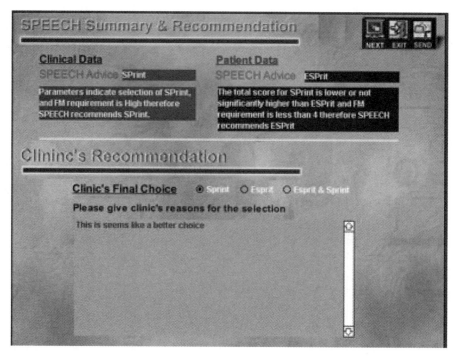

**Fig. 9.8**   Screen captures from 'Speech' showing the final screen where system's recommendations are presented to the user

months' evaluation and observation period was used to further modify and refine the package.

### 9.4.3   Case Study III

A Multimedia Book for 'Publish Everything'- A Global Publisher

**Initial project definition:** *'Publish Everything is a global publisher of business books. They have a project to publish a series of books that would suit MBA students. The first book in the series is on "Business Research Method" and the publisher also requires an accompanying CD-ROM that contains the textual material of the book as well as interactive features such as search and multimedia enhancements'*

**1. System Requirements:** This is a relatively straightforward and common type of project. We know that the system is a learning/training resource and the target users are MBA students. Further clarification of system requirements, through meetings with the client, determines that they require a multi-platform CD-ROM that runs both on PCs and Apple Macs. This helps us with the process of choosing the appropriate authoring tools to start the development work. Multimedia authoring

```
mouseUp

on mouseUp
  global Co
  set Co = 1
  set Zero = 0
  set Nin = 19
  set Eig = 18
  set Nit = 91
  put " " into member "sel1"
  if the text of member "ag" = " " then
    put "Please Enter Patient's Age" into member "er"
    startTimer
    repeat while the timer <120
    end repeat
    put " " into member "er"
    Set Co = 1
    ErMsg
  end if
  put the text of member "ag" into AG
  if value (AG) > value (Zero) and value (AG) < value (Nin) then
    put "1 - 18" into member "sel1"
    put "Age is: "& ag into line 3 of member "info"
    put Return&numToChar(10) into line 4 of member "info"
    put "SPrint" into member "ad1"
    put " " into member "cchoice"
    set the hilite of member "age1" = TRUE
    set Co = Co + 1
    set Sprint = Sprint + 1
  end if
```

**Fig. 9.9**   View of some of the Lingo code used to develop the inference engine

tools were discussed in Chapter 6. Macromedia's Director is a multi-platform tool that allows application development on both PCs and Apple Macs. The developer could choose either PC or Mac environment to develop the package.

**2. Design Considerations:** The project brief is such that some of the design decisions are already made. For example as we are required to develop an interactive multimedia book it is clear that the metaphor to be used is a book. The client provides the textual content, but to add the multimedia enhancements extensive media preparations are required. It is quite a common practice in large interactive multimedia system development projects that media preparations including voiceovers, video clips and animations are contracted out to media specialists. High quality digital video and voiceovers require a professional studio environment as well as sound and video engineering expertise.

   While it is clear that the bulk of the content provided is text based, nevertheless the extensive inclusion of video, audio and animation within the package requires careful media integration and synchronisation management. The navigational structure of the system is also very crucial. The client ideally requires a system that is simple to use and in terms of navigation could be easily handled by totally novice users.

**3. Visualising the User Interface:** Before starting the implementation of a prototype a series of storyboards depicting possible user interface designs were created and discussed with the client (Figure 9.10). Feedback from the client provided useful information before the actual implementation and prototyping could begin.

**4. Implementation:** Based on the decisions made during system requirement and design stages, a prototype version of the BRM was developed. The prototype was tested for possible programming bugs and then critically reviewed by both client and some MBA students allowing for further modifications to be made (Figures 9.11, 9.12, 9.13).

BRM's consistent menu structure also provides a very simple and yet effective navigational structure. The 'Control Panel' consists of five icons which are kept constant throughout the package. The icons provide functions such as getting back to the main menu, printing, viewing help and demo files as well as allowing the user to go to the index pages. The panel also contains additional navigation tools including forward, backward and back to point of origin (Figure 9.14). Furthermore, interactivity was also provided within the text area by creating hotspots that allowed branching and links to other parts of the package.

**5. Evaluation:** The 'BRM' system was using fifteen MBA students. The formative evaluation used observation methods to observe how the students used the package and then through questionnaires and one- to- one interviews with the students useful feed backs were obtained. Also summative evaluation was used to see how students compared the product with traditional books. Based on data gathered, further refinements and modifications were made before final mass production.


### 9.4.4   Case Study IV

A Corporate Image Presentation for a Multimedia Kiosk

**Initial project definition:** 'Company X is preparing a stand for a trade show. The company is a hi-tech electronic firm and plans to use touch screen multimedia kiosks to promote its products and services.'

**1. System Requirements:** This is another common application for interactive multimedia systems. Further details of the clients' requirements reveals that the multimedia package should be PC based. Furthermore, it is clear that multimedia kiosk and touch screen monitors are also required.

**2. Design Considerations:** The project brief provides enough clues about the nature and characteristics of the systems that need to be designed. The package is a presentation tool, so the client requires a self-running mode, as well as an interactive mode

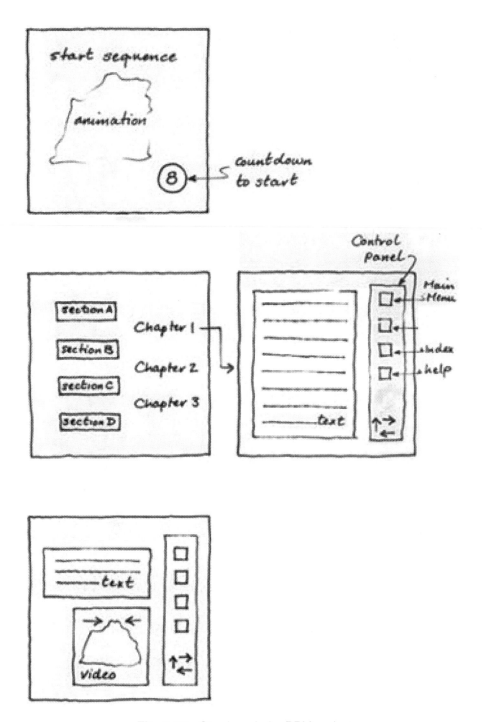

**Fig. 9.10**   Storyboards for BRM project

**Fig. 9.11**   View of opening screen of BRM package

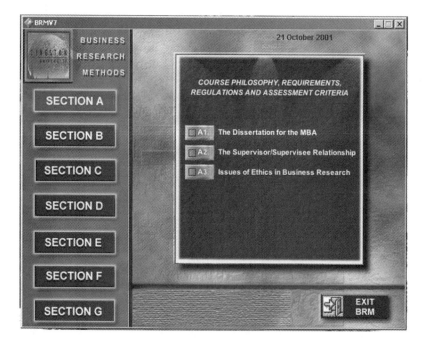

**Fig. 9.12**   BRM's Menu structure

**Fig. 9.13**   BRM's Multimedia enhancements – video clip playing

where users could stop the self-running mode and interact with the system. The client provides the product details including technical specifications and images. To add the multimedia enhancements again extensive media preparations are required. There are important decisions that the designer needs to make about the navigational structure of the system. A two-layered approach seems to be the solution to our problem. On one layer the system follows a set navigational path going through various screens. On the other layer the user could stop this process and explore the information manually. A useful metaphor often used for presentation types of packages is the movie metaphor where the user is treated like a passive viewer with little interaction allowed.

**3. Visualising the User Interface:** Before starting the implementation of a prototype a series of storyboards depicting possible user interface designs were created and discussed with the client (Figure 9.15). Feedback from the client provided useful information before the actual implementation and prototyping could began. As can be seen from the storyboards, a movie metaphor was used to design the user interface. This was particularly useful as part of the design consideration was a self-running mode where the system worked on its own without any user interaction.

**4. Implementation:** Based on the decisions made during system requirement and design stages a prototype version of the CD-ROM was developed. The prototype

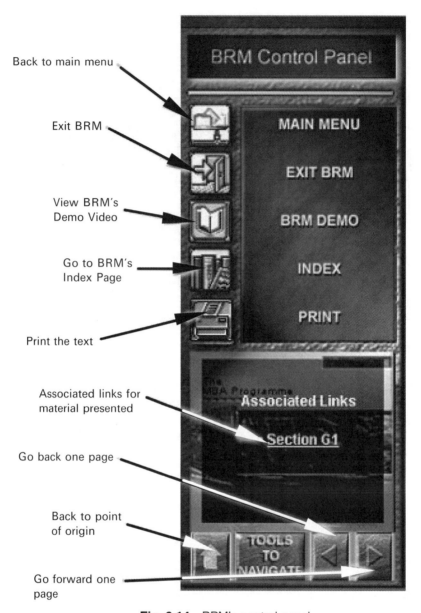

Back to main menu

Exit BRM

View BRM's
Demo Video

Go to BRM's
Index Page

Print the text

Associated links for
material presented

Go back one page

Back to point
of origin

Go forward one
page

**Fig. 9.14** BRM's control panel

was tested with both the touch screen monitor and the multimedia kiosk to make sure there are no practical problems. Figure 9.16 shows screen capture from the package.

**5. Evaluation:** The package was evaluated by the client to see if it met its stated aims and objectives.

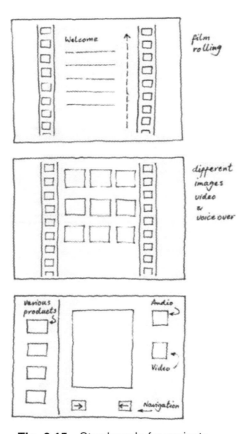

**Fig. 9.15**   Storyboards for projects

**Fig. 9.16**   Screen capture from the developed CD

As can be gathered from what we have discussed so far, design and development of interactive multimedia systems requires formal understanding of the software design process as well as a range of varying skills managing media preparations and integrations.

## Chapter Summary

- Almost all the different design models from the 'life cycle' model to prototyping, and even some of the object oriented design approaches view the process of designing software systems as going through a series of steps (commonly in an iterative manner). These common features and steps are:
  - Identifying the requirements of the system;
  - Identifying the design issues;
  - Implementation;
  - Testing and evaluation;
- Based on Shneiderman's proposed set of rules and the authors' practical experience, the following sets of guidelines are proposed for developing the user interface in an IMS:
  - Use of appropriate metaphor; Simplicity and ease of use; Consistency; the necessity for informative help and feedback and to provide mechanism for reversal of actions.

## Exercises and Projects

### PROJECT

Using an appropriate design and development process model design a Multimedia CD ROM title that could be used as a corporate identity tool for Fantastic Business School's new marketing drive.

The CD should introduce the school and give information on its postgraduate courses, the staff running the courses as well as the research centres based in the school. The CD should also contain the necessary information about how to get application forms and more information on individual courses.

**RECALL QUESTIONS**

1.   What are the key issues that need to be considered when designing the navigational structure of an IMS?
2.   The system requirement of the design covers what areas of concern for the designer?
3.   How could techniques like storyboarding be used to enhance the design process in terms of client feedback and interaction?

# 10

# A Brief Overview of Dierent Evaluation Methodologies

Knussen *et al.* (1991) point out that the two main categories of evaluations are *formative* and *summative*. Formative evaluation is concerned with progress towards achieving the goals of an innovation during its implementation. On the other hand summative evaluation is concerned with the effectiveness of an innovation on completion, in terms of the stated aims (Thorpe, 1988). In other words formative evaluation is best suited to ascertain whether products meet users' needs while summative evaluation is most appropriate in determining the suitability of a product compared to other or similar products already in use. The review of the literature shows different forms of formative and summative categories of evaluation. Lawton (1980) describes the following five forms or models of evaluation:

**1. The classical experimental model:** In the experimental model, it is assumed that control over all relevant experimental variables is both desirable and possible. The laboratory is the traditional setting for such evaluation. Knussen *et al.* (1991) point out that this approach may be followed when the outcome variable is clearly defined. They also noted that the results of such studies may prove irrelevant when the setting is the classroom. This model is useful for formative evaluations, quantitative measures and/or where comparisons could be made between various interactions of a particular system.

**2. The research and development (industrial) model:** The R&D model requires a clear indication of the objectives that are to be measured and appropriate pre and post tests. Many evaluations of CAL systems, especially those arising from computing science and industrial environment rather than educational environment, have adopted this model (Knussen *et al.* 1991).

**3. The illuminative model:** Parlett and Hamilton (1972) coined the term 'illuminative evaluation' to describe a qualitative approach that is based around observation and interviews. The illuminative method is particularly appropriate when the evaluator is trying to find out what happens to an innovation in practice. In this model, the emphasis is on illumination of important factors rather than the testing of a hypothesis. The illuminative model is also suitable for the study of individual differences. For example, the illuminative model could be used to investigate whether computer-based materials are more effective for some learners (or instructors) than others. O'Shea and T Self (1985), however, claims that there are a number of pitfalls with this method, the most important of which is that the illuminative approach is associated with subjective responses of people involved in the evaluation. He points out that the mere presence of an observer will have an effect on those being observed. Furthermore, as far as evaluating computer-aided learning is concerned, it is hard to imagine what observing learners using a particular computer package could achieve.

**4. The briefing decision-makers (political) model:** In this model political considerations on whether something is politically correct are taken into account and given more weight than adherence to pure methodology. MacDonald (1976) described this model as more akin to the illuminative than the experimental model in which evaluators need to be explicit about the values introduced into the evaluation process and about the way the results are then used. Knussen *et al.* (1991), commenting on the relevance of this type of evaluation for hypermedia, states that this model is less relevant than the illuminative and R&D models but it is useful in understanding the wider implications and meanings of evaluation. In their words, it allows the evaluator to consider the wider relevance or importance of an innovation.

**5. The case study model:** This model is used mainly in summative types of evaluation and is considered as appropriate in examining the effects of situational and personal factors.

Kirakowski and Corbett (1990) stated that the evaluation of human-computer interfaces should abide by more general methods applied to all forms of evaluation. However, the literature indicates that there are a number of guidelines that could be taken into account before an evaluation process starts. According to Kirakowski and Corbett (1990) these guidelines are:

- A conceptionalisation of the issues that need to be addressed.
- An indication of how the subject matter may be studied; and
- Ways of evaluating the results, which could lead to the integration of well-founded results into the activity of system design.

The debate presented above indicates that there are a variety of evaluation methods and approaches that could be adopted.

# Exercises and Projects

## RECALL QUESTIONS

1.  What are the two main types of evaluation and how do they differ?
2.  What are the assumptions made in the experimental model?
3.  Hamilton coined the term 'illuminative evaluation' to describe a qualitative approach discuss what the 'illuminative evaluation' could be used for.
4.  Knussen commented that the briefing decision-makers (political) model is appropriate for hypermedia evaluation. Discuss what type of evaluation this method could be used for.
5.  What are the guidelines that should be taken into account before an evaluation process starts?

# Part IV

# Internet, the World Wide Web, Distributed and Mobile Multimedia

*This section reviews the emergence of the Internet, and the World Wide Web. The Web is often viewed as a distributed multimedia environment, in this context, the delivery of multimedia on the Web is discussed and the final chapter of the book will glance into future and mobile multimedia.*

# 11

Internet, the World Wide Web and Issues in Delivering Multimedia Content on the Net

*'Radio was in existence 38 years before 50 million people tuned in; TV took 13 years to reach that benchmark. Sixteen years after the first PC kit came out; 50 million people were using one. Once it was opened to the general public, the Internet crossed that line in four years.' (From a report by the US Department of Commerce, 1994)*

## 11.1 BACKGROUND

Looking at the literature, which provides an account of the Internet's history, one cannot avoid stumbling on the suggestion that the emergence of the Internet in its current format was somehow more accidental than planned and its originators had no idea that their 'creature' would end up in its present shape and form.

Most books and papers written on the topic including a personal account by Vinton Cerf (1993),[1] suggest that the beginning of the Internet dates back to the 1960s. Some even have gone as far as pointing out that it was in 1957 following the Soviet Union's launch of the Sputnik satellite into orbit and the dawn of satellite communication, that led to the American administration, headed

---

[1] Vinton Cerf is one of the scientists who worked on the ARPA project when he was at UCL. See http://www.virtualschool.edu/mon/Internet/CerfHowInternetCame2B.html for the complete article.

by Eisenhower, seeking an appropriate response to this 'threat'. The questions being asked by various research organisations, at the time, including RAND, America's Cold War think-tank was: *'How could the US authorities successfully communicate after a nuclear war?'* As a result the US Department of Defence, sought to create a non-centralized network designed to survive partial nuclear war and still function when parts of the network were down or destroyed. Created by the Pentagon this project was called ARPANET (Advanced Research Projects Agency Network) with the aim of providing a secure and survivable communications network for organisations engaged in defence-related research. In 1962, Dr J.C.R. Licklider was chosen to head ARPA's research. In collaboration with private companies and universities Licklider laid the foundations for what later become the ARPANET.

In 1969, the first attempt to implement the original concept of long distance networked computers was organised. Four computers running on different sites were linked together by 50 Kbp circuits. The four computers forming the four nodes of the network were located in UCLA, Stanford Research Institute (SRI), UC Santa Barbara (UCSB), and the University of Utah in Salt Lake City. According to Kleinrock, a Professor of Computer science at UCLA, who with his team of students tried the first network connections across external sites: 'We set up a telephone connection between us and the guys at SRI . . . we typed the L and we asked on the phone, "Do you see the L?" "Yes, we see the L", came the response. We typed the O, and we asked, "Do you see the O'" "'Yes, we see the O." 'Then we typed the G, and the system crashed . . .' (*Sacramento Bee*, May 1, 1996)

In order to make the network global it was clear that standard protocols were needed and hence the IP (Internet Protocol) technology, which defines how electronic messages are packaged, addressed, and sent over the network, was developed. The full standard protocol was introduced in 1977 and was called TCP/IP (Transmission Control Protocol/Internet Protocol). TCP/IP allowed users to link various branches of other complex networks directly to the ARPANet, which soon came to be called the Internet.

The defence establishment eventually opted for MiliNet (dedicated to military research establishment) and dropped the ARPANet project, but ARPANet grew and was upgraded to a 'high speed' network by linking several powerful supercomputer stations called nodes. In 1985, the National Science Foundation (NSF) began a programme to establish Internet access across the United States.

Today, by Internet we refer to the global network of computers connected together using the TCP/IP technology. There is very little doubt that Internet has become a truly globally connected community or 'universe' with hundreds of millions of users exchanging information within its boundaries. According to the latest research carried out by Nielsen NetRatings (October 2001) the current 'Internet universe' in some of the leading industrial countries equals:

- 169.4 million users in USA
- 49.2 million in Japan
- 30 million in Germany
- 27.4 million in South Korea
- 24.3 million in UK

Although it is very difficult to give accurate figures for the number of users on the Internet it is clear that the Internet as a global communication medium where millions of people throughout the world log in to find information or buy consumer goods is growing at a phenomenal rate. Some estimate that by the year 2005 this universe will expand beyond the 1 billion users' mark with a business value of over 30 trillion dollars.

One of the questions I get asked quite often by students is, what is the relationship between hypertext, hypermedia, multimedia, and the Web? What has been discussed so far should have given strong indications to the reader, but in order to clarify things further let's briefly remind ourselves about a number of key issues.

We have already established that the term hypertext implied a system that deals only with text. With the integration of sound and video technology into the desktop PC and the emergence of MM systems, the term hypermedia has been used for hypertext systems that are capable of linking together more than just textual information. We further mentioned that therefore hypermedia can be viewed as the next development stage of hypertext. According to Encyclopedia Britannica 2002 the Web could be defined as:

> 'WWW, (byname THE WEB), is the leading information retrieval service of the Internet (the worldwide computer network). The Web gives users access to a vast array of documents that are connected to each other by means of hypertext or hypermedia links—i.e. hyperlinks, electronic connections that link related pieces of information in order to allow a user easy access to them.'

Furthermore, we mentioned before that multimedia is more than just multiple media. Multimedia adds interactivity to the combination of text, graphics, images, audio and video all under the control of desktop computer. Adding network to multimedia produces distributed multimedia (Agnew & Kellerman, 1996). Having established that hypermedia, as a concept, is the same as hypertext but in a multimedia environment, we could therefore conclude that the WWW is hypermedia environment, which is also distributed across a global network, i.e. the Internet. Amongst the potential application areas cited in the literature for distributed hypermedia systems one could mention the following:

- Global exchanges of information, which could contain media rich, content, i.e. electronic mails enhanced by audio and video; and
- Creation of new environments for business, education, entertainment and delivery of news and information.

## 11.2   THE WORLD WIDE WEB AND MARKUP LANGUAGES

Earlier in this chapter the reader was introduced to the definition that the Internet is a global network of computers connected together. To access and exchange the information stored on this global network we require special tools that would be compatible between different types of computers and operating systems. Hypertext, as a concept of organizing information using simple structure of nodes and links was the natural environment to be used. The most widely used system for hypertext access over the Internet is the World Wide Web (WWW).

As already mentioned in Chapter 3 it becomes clear that the WWW follows the three level architecture discussed in hypertext abstract machine model. The base level in this structure is the 'database level', which consists of all the servers on the Internet connected together and containing various types of information.

The servers are providers for the clients (users) who use a standardized format called HTML (Hypertext Markup Language) through a standard communication protocol called HTTP (Hypertext Transfer Protocol) to access the information.

The second level is the presentation level, which is handled by the client viewer running on user's machine (Nielsen, 1995). The combination of HTML & HTTP together resembles the model presented by the Hypertext Abstract Machine (HAM) and discussed in Chapter 3.

The next question that requires some clarification is what is a mark-up language and more specifically what do we mean by hypertext mark-up language. The origin of mark-up languages dates back to the early 1960s where a draft definition for GML (General Markup Language) was developed. Markup could be defined as way of defining the presentation of content in a document or more accurately everything in a document that is not content.

The original use of a general mark-up referred to handwritten instructions that the designer would write next to a document so that the typesetter could layout the document before it was sent for printing. The literature generally refers to two different types of mark-up: procedural and descriptive mark-up (Figure 11.1)

It was later in the 1980s that attempts were made to describe an international standard for mark-ups. The Standard Generalized Markup Language, or SGML, was published as an international standard (ISO 8879) in 1986. SGML contains a set of standards embedding descriptive mark-up within a document. SGML also specifies a standard method for describing the structure of a document. According to the World Wide Web consortium (www.w3c.org), the world wide body overseeing the development of Web, Tim Berners-Lee and Robert Caillau both working at CERN, an international high energy physics research centre near Geneva collaborated on ideas for a linked information system that would be accessible across different

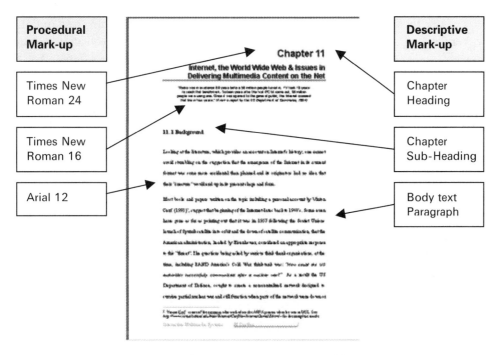

**Fig. 11.1**  Procedural and Descriptive Mark-up

computers. At that time many people were using TeX and PostScript for their documents. A few were using SGML. Tim Berners-Lee realised that something simpler was needed that would cope with dumb terminals through high-end graphical X Window workstations. HTML was developed as a simple solution, with a simple network protocol HTTP. CERN launched the Web in 1991 along with a mailing list called www-talk. The breakthrough came when the National Centre for Supercomputer Applications (NCSA) persuaded Marc Andersen and Eric Bina to develop the X Window Mosaic browser, which was later on available for both Apple and PC platforms, thus creating a graphic interface which since has become the common way of browsing through this hypertext world. According to W3C, HTML could be defined as:

> 'HTML is the lingua franca for publishing hypertext on the World Wide Web. It is a non-proprietary format based upon SGML, and can be created and processed by a wide range of tools, from simple plain text editors − you type it in from scratch- to sophisticated WYSIWYG authoring tools.'

Since its launch in 1991, HTML has gone through various versions, the latest being version 4.1.

Over the last few years the emphasis has shifted from developing and updating new versions of HTML to defining a more extensible and open structure where designers and developers could freely explore the possibilities offered by the technology. XML or eXtensiable Markup Language has emerged as the front-runner to implement such a vision. XML is extensible because it is not a fixed format like HTML (a single, predefined markup language). XML is actually a 'meta-language' a language for describing other languages. XML lets designers define their own customised markup languages for different classes of document. Current examples of these new emerging languages include MathML (Maths Markup Language), WML (Wap Markup Language) and SMIL (Synchronised Multi-media Integrated Language) covered in more detail later in this chapter.

## 11.3  ISSUES, TECHNOLOGIES AND TOOLS IN DEVELOPING DISTRIBUTED MULTIMEDIA APPLICATIONS ON THE WEB

The Web as a distributed multimedia environment is seen as a major area of application development. The complex nature and the diverse range of application areas means that inevitability a variety of technologies and tools are used to fulfill the potential offered by DMS. The range of enabling technologies and tools available offers services on two different levels. Firstly the client side (i.e. the environment where the user views when browsing) and secondly the server side (i.e. the backbone where all the data processing such as processing forms happen). The notable enabling technologies and tools include:

1. **Enabling Technologies**
   - Java
   - JavaScript
   - Common Gateway Interface
   - ASP (Active Server Pages)

2. **Tools**
   - Web Authoring Tools (client side)
   - E-Commerce Tools (client and server side)
   - Application Server Tools (server side)
   - Database Tools (mainly server side)
   - Management Tools (server side)
   - Search Tools (server and client side)
   - Security Tools (server side)
   - Multimedia Content Delivery Tools (client and server side)

While this section will give a brief overview of the range of tools available for developing DMS the main focus of this chapter will be on the multimedia content delivery, tools, techniques and design issues associated with it.

## 11.4    ENABLING TECHNOLOGIES

While the focus of this book is not about providing in depth discussion about the web and the growing range of enabling technologies that could be used in the design and development of interactive multimedia systems, nevertheless, the reader would benefit from a brief overview of these technologies. As mentioned earlier, the range of technologies are aimed at providing functionalities at two different levels.

The most notable technology that has emerged over the past seven years is Java℠. According to a white paper by Sun Microsystems, Java, whose original name was Oak, was developed as part of the Green project in Sun with the aim of producing a technology that could run across all platforms. From its early days in 1995, Java has grown to one of the most important technologies running across the web offering programmers the possibility of creating graphics, animations, and network functionalities. Java is a fully functional programming language that allows programmers to produce small pieces of code called Applets that could be accessed by web browsers.

One of the most widely used technologies in order to add interactivity on the client side, is JavaScript, which is also universally used as a scripting language across the web. Unlike some common misconception JavaScript has no relation to Java. JavaScript originally was called LiveScript and developed by Netscape Corporation and Sun Microsystems. Unlike Java, which requires a Java complier and needs to be complied before being accessed by web browsers, JavaScript code is written directly into an HTML file, which is then parsed by the browser. JavaScript allows developers to: control document appearance and content, control the browser, interact with the document content, interact with the users and manipulate embedded images. In summary, JavaScript could create: external windows, pop-ups, alerts, prompts and confirms, status bar enhancements, banner and tickers, cookies and search engines.

Unlike Java, JavaScript does not have any graphics capabilities, except for the ability to format and display HTML (which, could include images, tables, frames, forms, fonts, and other user-interface elements). Furthermore, JavaScript does not support networking of any kind, except allowing web browser to download the contents of arbitrary URLs. An example of JavaScript code displaying a Swap function, which is used in creating *Rollover* (i.e. when users' mouse is rolled over the specified image, the image is swapped with another image file) effect on a web page.

```
<html>
<head>
<title>Centre For Multimedia - Panel</title>
<meta http-equiv='Content-Type'
content='text/html; charset=iso-8859-1'>
```

```
<script language='JavaScript'> [where JavaScript
Starts]
<!--
function MM_swapImgRestore() { //v2.0
  if (document.MM_swapImgData != null)
for(var i=0; i<(document.MM_swapImgData.length-
1); i+=2) document.MM_swapImgData[i].src =
document.MM_swapImgData[i+1];
}
. . . . . . . . . . .
//-->
</script>    [where JavaScript Ends]
</head>
```

A number of web authoring tools (discussed later) like DreamWeaver and FrontPage allow designers to incorporate JavaScript codes within html pages without having an in-depth knowledge about JavaScript.

On the server side the key enabling technologies include Common Gate Interface (CGI) and Active Server Pages (ASP). CGI is part of the Web server that can communicate with other programmes running on the server. The idea is that each server and client program, regardless of the operating system platform, adheres to the same standard mechanism for the flow of data between client and server

Different programming languages, including C, C++, Perl, and TCL could be used to write CGI programs. Typical application areas for CGI includes form processing, image map manipulation, data base access, developing password protected areas . . . etc.

Active Server Page (ASP) is one of the Microsoft's web server application development technology. An ASP file is usually an HTML file, which includes scripts (like JavaScript) that are processed on a Microsoft Web server. ASP, like CGI is primarily a server-side scripting technology. The users on the client side do not have access to the actual scripts that implement the business logic, which is regarded as a main advantage ASP has over client-side scripting technologies. Like CGI, ASP code can be written in a number of scripting languages, including C, C++, Perl and JavaScript but the default scripting language for ASP is VBScript.

## 11.5 ENABLING TOOLS

### 11.5.1 Web Authoring Tools

**Macromedia Dreamweaver & Dreamweaver UltraDev.** Dreamweaver is a visual tool for professional Web site design. Dreamweaver allows Web designers to work in an

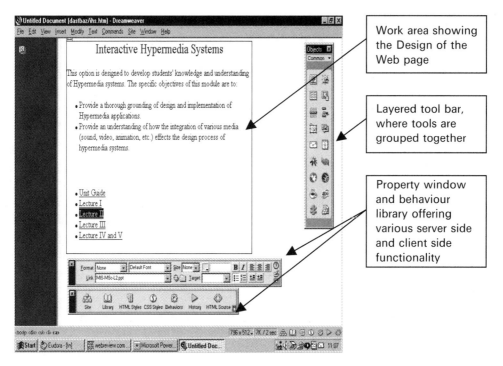

**Fig. 11.2**   A view from DreamWeaver's working environment

integrated environment where the designer could view code associated with a page as well as the output. Dreamweaver provides 'Roundtrip HTML' (according to Macromedia's documentation: Roundtrip HTML is a unique feature of Dreamweaver that lets you move your documents back and forth between a text-based HTML editor and Dreamweaver with little or no effect on the content and structure of the document's original HTML source code) and accelerate workflow with integration with Web applications, Microsoft Office, and e-commerce and application servers. Dreamweaver is one of the most popular tools used for Web authoring (for more information see: http://www.macromedia.com/).

**Adobe's GoLive:** which uses an icon-based interface, and offers an impressive breadth of design tools and technology support, including updated objects for inserting QuickTime, Flash, and SVG. Designers will appreciate GoLive's close ties to other Adobe graphics tools, and advanced Web developers will offers extended functionality (for more information see: http://www.adobe.com/products/golive/main.html).

**PageMill:** also offered by Adobe (but no longer available as it has been replaced by GoLive) offers integrated site management, giving users useful tools to manage their Web sites the way they want. Users can update graphics, links, text, animations and any other element across the entire site by simply dragging and dropping them (some information can be found at: http://www.adobe.com/products/pagemill/).

**HoTMetaL PRO:** A professional tool that provides users with more control over the Web development and management process. These include new FTP and remote file editing capabilities, improved handling of imported HTML source code, an improved drag and drop asset management system, and powerful new customization options (for more information see: http://www.hotmetalpro.com/).

**Microsoft's Front Page:** FrontPage is a tool that offers a lot of functionality but is heavily biased towards Microsoft's tool and vision of what the Web should be. While useful for the novice users most advanced Web designers and developers would find this very irritating. Front Page allows designers use of Dynamic HTML to animate, use of Cascading Style Sheets 2.0 to wrap or layer text and images, and get just the colours they want with enhanced colour tools. FrontPage also offers site management tools. FrontPage automatically fixes hyperlinks when files are renamed or moved (for more information see: http://www.microsoft.com/ms.htm).

**NetObjet Fusion:** Is a very useful and tool that allows users to quickly plan and build an entire site – with a consistent theme and formatting. The designer could benefits from comprehensive guidance, support, and knowledge base resources to help manage, promote, and grow the site. NetObject Fusion allows automatic create and updating of links, without writing code. It allows designers to choose from dozens of professional, customizable SiteStyles or create their own with drag-and-drop approach. (for more information see: http://www.netobjects.com).

A nice feature also offered on some of the tools mentioned above is the ability to provide links with databases for interactive Web applications and particularly e-commerce applications. Among some other tools that could be mentioned here are: HomeSite 4.5, HotDog Pro. Coral WebMaster, Claris HomePage, and CyberStudio.

### 11.5.2 E-Commerce Tools

Developing a fully functional e-commerce solution usually requires different tools to create: the 'Store Front', 'Shopping Carts', as well as 'Form Processing', 'Credit and Invoicing Processing' and 'Database facilities'. There are a number of tools available in the Market that can offer integrated e-commerce solutions, but these are usually expensive and also tie the designer to pre-defined sets of templates and designs. Among these type of tools the followings are worth mentioning:

**AuctionBuilder:** is a browser-based application for creating, customising, and administering auction sites (see Figure 11.3). AuctionBuilder features built-in auction layouts that are customisable by uploading images or using style templates. Auction-

**Fig. 11.3**   A view of AuctionBuilder's features

Builder includes built-in checksum verification for credit cards and support for secure (SSL) real-time payments (for more information see: http://www.ablecommerce.com/)

**DX Cart & DX Shop DXSHOP:**  provides everything a merchant needs to set up shop on the Internet. It includes: point and click shop design, necessary hosting product catalogue, system shopping cart system with shipping and tax calculator, secure server membership management system with affiliate tracking (for more information see: http://dgtconsulting.com/dxcart.html).

**xCommerce:** xCommerce consists of three different tools: Designer, Enterprise Enablers, and Server. xCommerce Designer is a visual design environment, targeted at business analysts and script-level programmers, that allows business information contained in XML documents to be rapidly integrated with other XML-formatted information (for more information see: http://www.techmatrix.co.jp/SilverStream/products/newlineup/xCommerce.html).

**DreamWeaver UltraDev:**  is the first authoring software that allows developers, programmers, and designers to visually create and edit data-driven web applications on multiple server platforms. Dreamweaver UltraDev generates applications that take advantage of Microsoft Active Server Pages (ASP), Sun Microsystems JavaServer

Pages (JSP), and Allaire ColdFusion mark-up language (CFML) technologies to connect to industry standard servers.

### 11.5.3  Management Tools

Management tools provide various key information that are used for both mainten-ance and updating of large distributed multimedia systems on the Web. Among the range of technologies and functionalities are: Feedback; Tracking; Server Security; Maintenance & Up-keep; Site Statistics and Viewer Information; Marketing & Profiling Tools. Delivering decision support information for Web site optimisation enhancement to the Internet presence, as well as providing a measure of website functionality make these group of tools a necessity for large Web development. Analysing server's LOG file, which contains valuable information about how many people, visited a site and more importantly what they did during their visit provides marketing departments with key information to adopt new marketing strategy or refine existing ones. Some of the better-known tools in this category are:

**Webfeedback:** Using graphics representation, webfeedback provides useful informa-tion on a web site functionality as well as useful information about Web site optimisa-tion and the enhancement of your Internet presence. Webfeedback tracks the strengths and weaknesses of the website and is also an indicator for assessing return on Internet investment (for more information see: www.liebhart.com/webfeedback/).

**Macromedia Aria:** Is another graphic based tool that by identifying high-value data and quickly delivering focused reports, provides intelligent management data to manage an e-business and gain a deep understanding of how specific visitors react to: affiliated promotions, product sales tactics, and advertising (Aria has recently been replaced with Macromedia's new ColdFusion suite see: http://www.macromedia.com).

**WebTrend's Analysis suite:** provides insightful information on web visitor behaviour, providing detail reporting on visitors' behaviour during their visit (see Figure 11.4). It also provides information on how visitors get to your site and the pages where they spend their time (for more information see http://www.webtrends.com/products/).

### 11.5.4  Search and Database Tools

These are tools that allow Web masters to add full-text search capabilities to a Web site. Search engines are a crucial tools used in all sort of Web environments. Some search engine providers like 'Excite' and others allow the use of their customized search engine on sites. Beside these there are tools available for developing customi-sable search engines.

Database connectivity is arguably one of the most important application areas that Web developers need to be aware of. More and more Web sites need to be

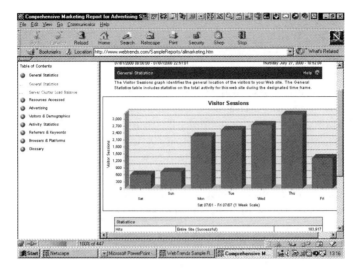

**Fig. 11.4**   A view from Web Trend and Analyser

connected to large databases that are dynamically updated (like product catalogues etc.) and handle large amount of information. One of the best-known tools used for professional application development is Oracle. Oracle can deliver unprecedented ease-of-use, power, and performance. Oracle also includes a fully integrated set of management tools, full distribution, replication, and integrated Web features. Replication and distributed data-access features allow users to share relational data across applications and servers. Furthermore, the built-in Web capabilities enable complete, intranet-computing solutions.

## 11.6   DELIVERING MULTIMEDIA CONTENT ON THE WEB

Although the Web started its life as a mainly text-based environment, the use of multimedia content in the form of graphics, animation, audio and video has transformed the nature of the Web and has posed interesting questions for Web designers and developers. As already discussed in part 2 and 3 of this book, to design and develop interactive multimedia systems, the designer requires a whole range of skills including understanding how to work with audio and video and the wide range of tools available for their manipulation.

While text and graphics could be easily incorporated into a Web site using native tools, such as hypertext markup language, and the scripting facilities available through JavaScript and Common Gateway Interface (CGI) the inclusion of audio, video and animation requires specialist tools.

The most common types of graphics used across the web are GIF and JPEG files (discussed in detail in Chapter 4). These file formats are the default types for all the browsers including Microsoft's Internet Explorer and Netscape Navigator. Another Common type of graphic file used across the web is the GIF animation file. These are small-animated graphics that can be seen by the browsers. This is sometimes referred to as GIF89a-based animation for the Web. As well as dedicated Gif animation tools that could be found on various shareware libraries on the Web a number graphic tools such as Adobe's PhotoShop would allow the creation of Gif animations by creating a number of drawings and then putting them together as frames, with time delay and other transition effects added between frames.

The initial approach to inclusion of audio, video and animation on the web was placing these types of files on the Web server and then providing links to them from a Web page. By clicking the link the user would then start the 'downloading' of the file from its location on the server to its local computer. This method, considering that most people accessing the web are using modems that at best are only capable of achieving 56 Kb data transfer rate would have meant that the downloading a 1 minute video clip could have taken a long time (up to one hour) and hence not a practical option. The emergence of streaming technology as well as advancement of compression techniques have provided Web designers with solutions to long download times and hence we have seen an explosion in the use of these technologies on the Web.

Beside the streaming technology, which will be discussed in more detail, html could be used to embed small audio files using the standard *wav* and *midi* format. Here is an example of including a digital sound file:

```
<html>
<head>
<title>Untitled Document</title>
<meta http-equiv='Content-Type'
content='text/html; charset=iso-8859-1'>
</head>
<BODYWIDTH=239 HEIGHT=108 BGCOLOR='#FFFFFF'
TEXT='#000000' LINK='#0000FF' VLINK='#ff0000'
ALINK='#00ff00'>
<center><font color='0000ff'><b>
Welcome To MY SOUND
Gallery!</b></font></CENTER>
<EMBED src='LOGOSND.wav' width=2 height=2
ALIGN=ABSBOTTOM AUTOSTART=true
LOOP=false></embed>
<H2> Testing Digital Sound <BR>
The Sound Should Start Automatically
```

```
</H2>
</body>
</html>
```

### 11.6.1  Audio and Video Streaming?

Streaming audio is the sound that is delivered to the user as it is being received from the Web site that you are visiting. The audio file is broken up into small pieces (streams) and then sent from the server to the client's machine, the browser on the client's machine uses a helper application (like RealAudio) to re-assemble the audio stream. This is different from downloading a file to a hard drive and then playing it after the entire file has been downloaded. The advantage of streaming is that there is usually no waiting (or very little) from the time the mouse is clicked until the time the sound starts playing. The same approach could be used to stream video files across the Web. According to recent reports published, the streaming technology industry is the fastest growing industry on the net and this trend is expected to continue and grow. The key providers, as far as streaming technology is concerned are: Real Networks, Apple and Microsoft.

RealAudio is a streaming audio technology developed by Real Networks. The RealAudio player (the client software) is available for free from Real Networks' Web site. RealAudio is capable of sending audio files in two different formats:

1.    Stereo 8 KHz sampling rate for 28.8 kbs connections ($\sim$2.5 KB/sec.) and
2.    Stereo 16 KHz sampling rate for 56+ kbs connections ($\sim$5 KB/sec.).

Another emerging technology in creating audio content for the web is the use of compression techniques and namely MP3. (See Chapter 4 for more details.) In order to create streaming audio or video files, the multimedia designer firstly needs to create the digital audio or video file format (acceptable file formats are .wav, .aif, .avi, .mov, .mpg) and then using a RealAudio producer or similar type of software the digital file format is broken into streams ready for broadcasting over the Internet. Figure 11.5.

### 11.7    ANIMATION ON THE WEB

The reader has already been introduced to the concept of animation in Chapter 5. There are different ways of creating animation for the Web. As already mentioned we could use programming techniques by using Java or alternatively use high level tools like Macromedia's Flash (Figure 11.6).

Also Movies created in Macromedia's Director could be saved (and compressed) as Shockwave files and played back within the browser environment using Shockwave plug-in. Playing Flash animation also requires Flash plug-in.Flash which

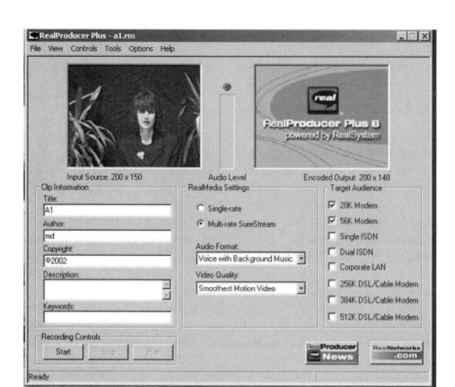

**Fig. 11.5** A view from RealProducer V.8 working environment

is the most popular high-end application development tool for creating animations is quite similar to Director in terms of its metaphor (creating movies) and its components (scoreboard, sprites, etc.). The main components of a Flash movie are primarily vector graphics, but they can also contain imported bitmap graphics and sounds. Flash movies allow multimedia designers to incorporate interactivity to permit input from viewers, and allow the creation of non-linear movies that can interact with other Web applications. Flash movies are compact and small in size, so they download rapidly and scale to the viewer's screen size (Figure 11.7).

## 11.8  SYNCHRONISED MULTIMEDIA INTEGRATED LANGUAGE (SMIL)

According to W3C

> 'The Synchronized Multimedia Integration Language (SMIL, pronounced 'smile') enables simple authoring of interactive audiovisual presentations. SMIL is typically used for 'rich media'/multimedia presentations which integrate streaming audio and video with images, text or any other media type. SMIL is an easy-to-learn HTML-like language, and many SMIL presentations are written using a simple text-editor.'

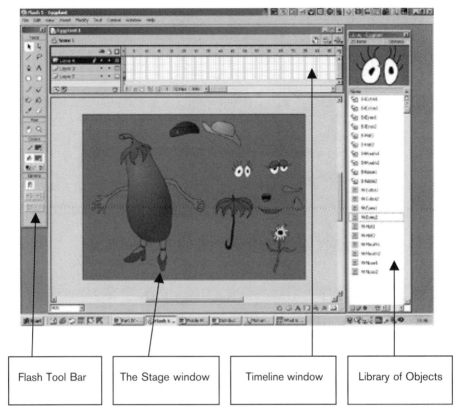

**Fig. 11.6**   Flash's working environment

With the introduction of Synchronized Multimedia Integration Language (SMIL) in 1999, multimedia creators were presented with a tool for designing and developing time-based, streaming multimedia presentations that combine audio, video, images, and text. SMIL is an XML-based language that allows control over the what, where, and when of media elements in a multimedia presentation with a simple, clear markup language similar to HTML. With the latest version of SMIL (version 2) released in August 2001, the full integration of multimedia within native hypertext markup language took a step closer. SMIL 2 adds functionality to web environment in ten areas. These include:

1.   Timing
2.   Time manipulations
3.   Animation
4.   Content control
5.   Layout

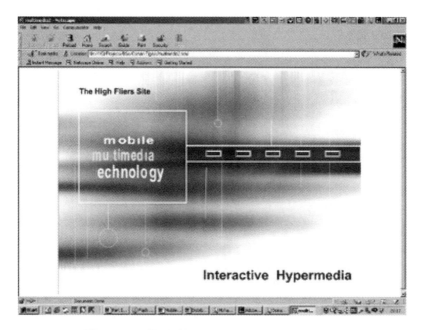

**Fig. 11.7** Flash Movie playing in Web browser

6. Linking
7. Media objects
8. Meta information
9. Structure and
10. Transitions

At the heart of SMIL structure is the <switch> tag, which is the mechanism used to enable the client's browser to make informed decisions about the presentation. The <switch> tag could also operate similar to the concept of 'If...Else' statement found in traditional programming languages which will allow branching operations. For example the <switch> tag could be used to check the Internet connection of a client and the speed by which data could be transferred. Here is an example

```
<switch>
      <par systemBirate = 56000'>
      ...
      </par>
      <par systemBirate = 9600'>
      ...
      </par>
</switch>
```

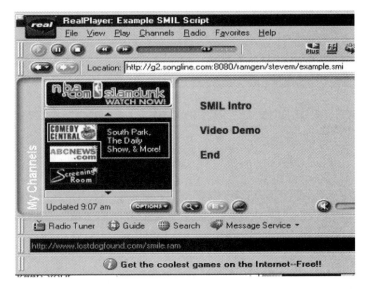

**Fig. 11.8**   SMIL file running on RealAudio player

Another interesting feature in SMIL is the way it handles links. SMIL uses the <A> and <Area> tags to create links. The <A> tag creates a direct link from a node to any part of another document. The <Area> tag allows the multimedia designer to create a direct link from an area of an image, or video, to any part of another document.

Viewing SMIL files are still an issue not completely resolved. Although Microsoft has promised support for SMIL file format in the future release of Internet Explorer, but not to version 5.5 SMIL file formats would only be viewed through RealAudio player. Let's have a look at an SMIL example.

```
<smil>
<head>
<layout><!--- Main Window Setting -- >
<root-layout
height = '550'
width = '550'
backgroundColor = 'black' />
<region id = 'Region0'
backgroundColor = '#602030'/>
<region id = 'Region1'
backgroundColor = '#602030'
fit = 'fill'
width = '500'
height = '550'
</layout>
```

```
</head>
...
</body>
```

## 11.9  ISSUES IN DESIGN OF INTERACTIVE MULTIMEDIA SYSTEMS ON THE WEB

In Chapter 5 and six various design approaches as well as a number of design and development case studies were presented to readers. I would like to argue that general design principles discussed for developing interactive multimedia systems hold true for developing such systems for the Web. Nielsen (2000), raises an interesting point about designing usable Web sites. According to him there are two basic approaches to designing Web sites. The artistic ideal of expressing ideas and the engineering model of solving problems for the customers. He goes on to emphasise that his book 'Designing Web Usability' is firmly on the side of engineering. Although this approach undoubtedly has its merits and the HCI academic community strongly recommends this approach, there is no reason that we could not argue for successful mixing of both artistic approaches with an engineering one. Nielsen (2000) quiet correctly points out that despite the common view held that the dominant metaphor for the web is Television and hence the use of words likes 'channel', 'casting', 'show' etc. the web is not like television at all. Web like other multimedia information systems is user driven and therefore requires being highly interactive. The following steps could be used in starting the design process. Let's look at following example:

**The Brief:** The School of Computing of X-University requires a Web site to advertise their courses and other useful information about the school and to have interactive features such as requesting information packs etc.

**Possible steps:**
1.   Further clarify and define Objectives of the Site (i.e. what is the main purpose of the site, what information should be presented, the technology/technologies required for the site, i.e. Form processing, Animation, Security, etc. future maintenance and expansion plans.)
2.   Produce a rough flow chart of the Web site with all the layers and as much detail as possible
3.   Design a prototype for testing
4.   Test functionality and design features with clients.
5.   Implement the site.

A typical design (flow) chart for the site is presented in Figure 11.9.

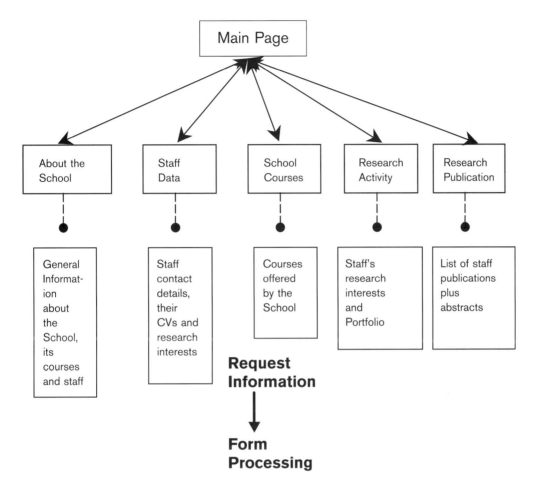

**Fig. 11.9**  A possible Design (Flow) chart for the Site

Other considerations that need to be taken into account as good design principles are as follows:

1.  Good navigational structure (i.e. appropriate link structure allowing users to easily get back to their point of origin).
2.  Clear content presentation, avoiding cluttering of pages with graphics that serve no purpose.
3.  Avoiding outdate information and broken links (links that no longer work).
4.  Creating relationship between the text and various elements within the page.
5.  Using appropriate contrast between elements within a page creating visual attraction.

6.    Ensuring consistency throughout the site in terms of use of colours, graphics and particularly interactive icons.

7.    Using ALT tags to provide users with information about links. This is particularly important for people with a disability.

8.    Avoiding *Frames* at all costs. A key problem to note on the use of frames is that most search engines on the web ignore pages with frames and hence make these pages very difficult to be found on the web.

9.    Providing site maps to give as much support information as possible to site visitors.

10.   If multimedia enhancements or content are present, always provide users with information and choice about their use and therefore provide them with simple text alternatives.

11.   Promote use of style sheets, particularly for large web site developments, as style sheets are useful mechanism to create a consistent style for the entire Web site.

12.   Check spelling of the content as well as making sure that the information presented is accurate and correct.

13.   Avoid arbitrary loading and looping of animations or sound, as most Web users find this very annoying.

14.   Avoid blinking text.

15.   Make sure each page within the site have correct titles and headings.

16.   Carefully consider the use of appropriate meta tags for your Web pages, which will be, extremely useful to search engines indexing information about your site.

While there are different approaches and views about what good web design is all about, the author agrees with the view that:

> *'Web sites should make the main things users want to do very simple. Other actions and advanced features can certainly be possible but simple things should be simple to do.'*

> (Nielsen, 2000).

## Chapter Summary

- In 1969, the first attempt to implement the original concept of long distance networked computers was organised. Four computers running on different sites were linked together by 50 Kbp circuits.
- Today, by Internet we refer to the global network of computers connected together using the TCP/IP technology. There is very little doubt that

Internet has become a truly globally connected community or 'universe' with hundreds of millions of users exchanging information within its boundaries.

- The original use of a general mark-up referred to handwritten instructions that the designer would write next to a document so that the typesetter could layout the document before it was sent for printing.
- Although the Web started its life as a mainly text-based environment, the use of multimedia content in the form of graphics, animation, audio and video has transformed the nature of the Web and has posed interesting questions for Web designers and developers.

## Exercises and Projects

### PROJECT

A PC hardware company intends to set up an E-Commerce Web site. The company wants the site to be used as its "Store Front" where customers could visit, check various products and promotions, and then place an order.

The company also requires intelligent management data regarding number of customers and how various promotions are being received.

Discuss the range of tools and technologies required carrying out these activities.

### RECALL QUESTIONS

1. Discuss six different considerations that need to be taken into account as good design principles for designing an interactive Web site.
2. what is SMIL and how it could be used in delivering multimedia content on the WWW?
3. What are the differences between SGML, XML and HTML? What is meant by DTD?
4. Discuss the differences between procedural and descriptive mark-up.
5. How could streaming technology be used for the delivery of multimedia content on the World Wide Web.

# 12

# Mobile Multimedia: A Glance into the Future

*'The beginning is the most important part of the work.' Plato*

## 12.1 BACKGROUND

The emerging communications, electronics, and computer technologies are creating a new multimedia fabric for the decades to come. The nature of this new fabric is still evolving and the reality is that, at present, we have more searching questions than concrete answers.

The buzzword being splashed around is *Convergence* and by it we mean the convergence of multimedia technology with the telecommunications industry. If, for example, features of the telephone and television are combined, the resultant is a visually enriched communication tool that makes applications such as home shopping, distance learning, remote collaboration with specialists, and interactive access to live and stored video sources around the world possible.

Many believe that the nature of the current technological changes is based on consumerism, fuelled by mass advertising by large corporations such as Sony and Nokia promoting 'live style' goods such as the latest phones and MP3 players. According to a WAP[1] forum report, there will be more than 530 million wireless subscribers by the end of the year 2001. New estimates report that the number of wireless subscribers will break the one billion mark by 2004, and a 'substantial portion of the phones sold this year will have multimedia capabilities.'

Despite the big advertising push by telecommunication companies, the integration of multimedia with mobile computing presents many challenges to wireless

---

[1] WAP stands for Wireless Application Protocol and will be discussed later in this chapter.

service providers, application developers and manufacturers. There are fundamental issues which need to be considered, including problems with viewing information on very small screens, the dismal bandwidth available on the first and second generation of mobile devices and so on. We are even struggling to find a common platform to define what mobile multimedia technology is about and whether there are any realistic and worthwhile applications for them.

## 12.2 MOBILE MULTIMEDIA TECHNOLOGY

The most common definition offered in the extant literature is to say that mobile multimedia could be considered as the emergence of multimedia computer systems that are both mobile in that they are capable of being integrated into the telecommunications and networking infrastructures and offer access to services and applications using combinations of data, text, voice, video (among others) to anybody, anytime, anywhere.

The history of creating wireless communication devices dates back to Marconi's attempt in introducing wireless communication in 1895. It was however in the early 1980s that the first generation of cellular systems appeared in the U.S. These systems were called Advanced Mobile Phone Systems and operate in the 824–849 MHz and 869–894 MHz bands. At the same time, in Europe, similar systems called NMT (Nordic Mobile Telephone System), were developed which operated on 450 and 900 MHz bands. These systems use FM (Frequency Modulation) modulation for speech and in-band signalling. These first generation systems were primarily designed for speech transmission. However, some experiments of data and low bit rate video transmission over these systems had taken place (Furht, 1999).

The second-generation of mobile communication emerged soon afterwards, commonly referred to as GSM (Global System for Mobile Communications). GSM is based on digital time division multiplexing and has a raw data rate of 13.8 kbps (with error checking this is reduced to 9.6 kbps). GSM as a mobile network standard in the context of wireless multimedia is, simply, a technically sophisticated radio communications network offering mobility and supporting wireless information services/ highways (Furht, 1999).

Approximately just over half of the world's digital subscribers are on networks based on the GSM standard, with the majority situated in Europe and in Asia. GSM networks are based on circuit switching. Once a connection is established, the user has the exclusive access to a certain amount of bandwidth until the connection terminates. As well as voice calls, 2G phones can also send and receive data, so they can provide limited data services such as text messaging and Wireless Application Protocol (WAP) browsing using micro-browsers. Most mobile phones in use today are the second-generation (2G) mobile phones or the enhanced 2.5G version, which offers improved data capabilities, such as higher transmission rates and 'always-on-connection'.

While Europe has been concentrating on GSM, the USA and Japan have been developing their own technologies. According to the *Financial Times* September 2000, NTTDoCoMo, the largest cellular operator in Japan, has successfully introduced i-mode to Japan, which is a rival technology to WAP based on CHTM a condensed version of HTML. By the start of September 2000, i-mode had more than 11 million subscribers compared to the world population of WAP which is probably not more than a fifth of this total. I-Mode is a wireless technology offering wireless web browsing and email from mobile phones. It enables users to access Internet services via their wireless phones. This technology is based on packet data transmission and thus is 'always-online. This means that users are charged only for the amount of information they retrieve and not for the time they spend using it.

If we are to believe the handset manufacturers, the future has already arrived. Japan has started testing the new generation of mobile devices capable of full multimedia content delivery and despite early mishaps the future, looks promising. The manufacturers are predicting that by the year 2005 there could be 5 billion mobile subscribers. The Third-generation (3G) mobile are capable of much higher data rates measured in Mbps and are intended for applications other than voice – such as mobile games. The 3G systems promise to offer higher speeds and 'always-on' data connections. It will also support heavy bandwidth hungry multimedia applications such as full-motion video; video-conferencing and advanced data services with full Internet access. The 3G networks are also designed to support large numbers of users more efficiently than 2G networks and allows for future expansion. Universal Mobile Telecommunication Service (UMTS) system is also another key emerging technology which is due to replace GSM. UMTS is a 3G standard supporting a theoretical data transfer rate of up to 2 Mpbs will possibly be launched globally by 2005 (source: Nokia) (Figure 12.1).

Another very interesting technology that has emerged over the last few years is the *Bluetooth* technology. According to IEEE's *Multimedia* magazine, September 2000, Bluetooth is not a rival technology to WAP but a technology, which can complement the Wireless Application Protocol. Bluetooth is a short-range radio technology designed to simplify peer-to-peer connectivity. It enables mobile phones, printers, PCs and PDAs to communicate directly with each other at high speeds without the need for a network server or cables. As Bluetooth uses radio transmission, it transfers voice and data in real-time. According to the same source, there is one possible snag to this standard. It operates in the 2.4 GHz frequency band, which is not part of the mobile network frequency. This frequency is freely available worldwide except for France, where the French military has rights to a large part of the radio spectrum, including the 2.4 GHz Bluetooth uses.

**Fig. 12.1**   Nokia's 3G Vision

While these rapid developments are taking place, designers and multimedia developers pause to ask the question. Are there any worthwhile application areas for the new emerging technology? According to a WAP forum report, presented to WAP Sydney, Australia in May 2001, there are emerging applications areas including:

- M-commerce: shopping, ticket purchases, reservations, and comparison shopping.
- Finance: statements, funds transfer, and shares trading.
- M-billing: notification, presentation and payment of bills
- Enterprise Access: inventory, shipment/sales updates, and email access
- M-care: customer service, payment status, and other backroom operations
- Entertainment: games, gambling, and interactive multi-player events
- Messaging: communication and collaboration
- Travelling: scheduling, reservations and advisories.

Entertainment and m-commerce are seen as key application areas for the emerging technology. Mobile entertainment covers a range of applications, including video,

**Fig. 12.2**  Media Screens – Nokia's vision of future mobile entertainment devices

audio, games and betting. While today very simple entertainment systems exist, it is likely that much more complex applications will be available in the future, enabling users to develop chat groups, play interactive games, download books and stream audio and video files to their handheld devices. Another important development is the delivery of streaming Video to mobile devices and TV-mobiles. Companies are already working on streaming video over mobile devices. Samsung launched a mobile phone handset with a built-in miniature TV at the Sydney Olympics. This phone has a special antenna capable of receiving both phone signals and TV transmissions. The TV can be viewed for up to 200 minutes on a single battery charge. If a phone call arrives when the TV facility is on, the screen automatically switches to the phone mode (Figure 12.2).

So what sort of mobile multimedia future awaits us? Barnes and Noble recently announced that it would sell an e-book device from Nuvomedia which will enable users to download books from the web. A Norwegian firm, Screen Media, will release a Linux-based e-book with built-in wireless connectivity and eventually, people should be able to download personalised newspapers and books from the Internet to read on the move.

I am not sure if we are yet ready for such a future, but one thing is for sure and that is that the multimedia technology has changed our lives beyond recognition. The new generation of children growing up in the multimedia age, with their multimedia mobile games consoles are all embracing the technology that is dazzling them, this in sharp contrast to the generation that by its historical experience is very cautious and slow to accept such drastic and unsettling changes.

## Chapter Summary

- The buzzword being splashed around is Convergence and by it we mean the convergence of multimedia technology with the telecommunications industry.
- The most common definition offered in the extant literature is to say that mobile multimedia could be considered as the emergence of multimedia computer systems that are both mobile in that they are capable of being integrated into the telecommunications and networking infrastructures and offer access to services and applications using combinations of data, text, voice, video (among others) to anybody, anytime, anywhere.
- The Third-generation (3G) mobiles are capable of much higher data rates measured in Mbps and are intended for applications other than voice – such as mobile games. The 3G systems promise to offer higher speeds and 'always-on' data connections.
- Bluetooth is a short-range radio technology designed to simplify peer-to-peer connectivity. It enables mobile phones, printers, PCs and PDAs to communicate directly with each other at high speeds without the need for a network server or cables.

## Exercises and Projects

### PROJECT

This is a group project aimed at carrying out extensive research on emerging Mobile Multimedia technology and its various application areas. The research should cover some or all of the following areas such as:

- Emergence of Mobile Multimedia
- Hardware & Software development of Mobile Multimedia systems
- Development of the Communication Industry
- Emergence of WAP and how its application areas
- Current trends within the Mobile Multimedia technology and its future directions

### RECALL QUESTIONS

1.  What are the differences between G1, G2, G2.5 and G3 technologies?

2.   What is WML and how does it differ from HTML and SGML?
3.   What are the key differences between I-Mode and GPRS technologies?
4.   Discuss some of the key application areas for the emerging mobile multi-media technology.
5.   What is UMTS and which technologies is it aiming to replace?

# Multimedia Bibliography

*The following is a list of references that I have gathered during the last eight years of research on Multimedia systems and the use of multimedia technology in learning and teaching. They include the references I have used in this book as well as the ones I have not used but nevertheless would be beneficial to the reader.*

Abboud, C.V. and Bunderson, C.V (1971); 'A computer assisted instruction program in the Arabic writing system'; *Technical Report No. 4*, CAL Laboratory, University of Texas at Austin.

Abraham, E., Loughrey, C. and Whalen, H. (1987); 'Computerised practice set in introductory financial accounting'; *Issues in Accounting Education*, Spring, pp. 1–12

Agnew, P. and Kellerman, A. (1996); 'Distributed Multimedia – Technologies, Applications and Opportunities in the Digital Information Industry'; Addison Wesley Publishing.

Akscyn, R.M., McCracken, D.L. and Yoder, E.A. (1988); 'A distributed hypertext for managing knowledge in organisation'; *Communications of the ACM*, **31**(7).

Aukstakalnis, S., and Blatner, D. (1992); 'Silicon Mirage The Art and Science of Virtual Reality'. Berkeley, California: Peachpit Press, Inc

Ambrose, D.W (1991) 'The effects of hypermedia on learning: A literature review'; *Educational Technology*, December.

Anderson, J.R. and Bower, G.H (1973); '*Human associative memory*'; New York: Wiley and Sons Publishers.

Anderson, B. (1994); 'Cognitive anthropology and user-centred system design I: how to enter and office'; *LUTCHI Internal Report No. 94/M/LUTCHI/0162*.

Ausubel, D.P. (1968); '*Educational psychology: A cognitive view*'; New York: Holt Rinehart and Winston.

Avison, B. *et al.* (1994); 'Information systems development: Methodologies, techniques and tools'; Alfred Waller Ltd.

Baecker, R.M. and Buxton, W.A.S. (1990); 'An historical and intellectual perspective' [of HCI]; In J. Preece and L. Keller (eds.) *Human-computer interaction*; Hemel Hempstead: Prentice Hall Publishers.

Barfield, L. (1993); '*The user interface – concepts and design*'; Reading, Mass: Addison Wesley Publishers.

Bartolome, A.R. and Sandals, L. (1996); 'Evaluating educational multimedia programmes in North America'; *Proceedings of Educational Multimedia and Hypermedia 1996*; AACE Publications.

Baumgartner, P. and Payr, S. (1996); 'Learning as a action of social science approach to the evaluation of interactive media'; *Proceedings of ED-MEDIA 1996*, June, Boston USA.

Beagoray, J.A (1990); 'An introduction to hypermedia issues, systems and application areas', *International Journal of Man – Machine Studies* 33.

Beard, R. and Hartley, J. (1984); '*Teaching and learning in higher education*'; 4th edition, New York: Harper Education Series.

Bennett, J.L. (1979); 'The communication impact of usability in interactive systems'; In Shackel, B. (ed.) *Man-Computer communication: Infotech state of the art*, vol. 2, Infotech International, London.

Bennett, S., McRobb, S. and Farmer, R. (1999); 'Object Oriented Systems Analysis and Design'; McGraw Hill Publishing.

Bell, K.R. and Scobie, G.E.W. (1992); 'MM technology, banks and their customers'; *International Journal of Bank Marketing*, **10**(2).

Bell, D. (2000); 'Software Engineering – A Programming Approach'; Addison Wesley Publishing.

Bevilacqua, A. F. (1989); 'Hypertext: behind the hype.'; *American Libraries*, **20**(February).

Bennett, S., Priest, A. and Macpherson, C. (1999); 'Learning about online learning: an approach to staff development for university teachers'; *Australian Journal of Educational Technology*, **15**(3).

Bjorkander, M. 'Graphical Programming Using UML and SDL'; *Journal of J-Computer*, Vol. **33**, No. 12

Blackman, D. (1980); 'Images of man in contemporary behaviourism'; In Chapman, D. and Jones, C. (eds.) *Models of Man*, London: British Psychological Society.

Bleber, M. and Isakowitz, T. (1995); 'Editorial of the Special Issue of the Communications of the ACM devoted to Hypermedia'; *Communications of the ACM*; **38**(8).

Bloomfield, H. (1994); '*Links in hypertext: an investigation into how they can provide information on inter-node relationships*'; Unpublished PhD. Queen Mary and Westfield College, University of London.

Bobbitt, B.J. (1992); '*Building the electronic shopping mall: A multimedia architecture for electronic commerce*', PhD thesis, UMI Publications.

Bork, A. (1989); '*The history of computers and education*'; Educational Technology Centre, Irvine: University of California.

Borthick, F. and Clark, L. (1986); 'The role of productive thinking in affecting student learning with microcomputers in accounting education', *Journal of Accounting Review*, **11**(1).

Boyle, T. (1997); '*Design for multimedia learning*'; Hemel Hempstead: Prentice Hall Europe Publications.

Braude, A. (1992); 'Computers in creative: Betting on the future'; *Advertising Age*, **63**(5).

Brittan, C. *et al.* (2000); 'Object-Oriented systems development: A gentle introduction'; McGraw Hill publishers.

Brown, P.J. (1991); 'Hypertext: dreams and reality'; In Brown, H. (ed.), *Hypermedia/Hypertext*, New York: Chapman & Hall.

Brown, R. (1992); 'Putting MM to the test'; *Systems 3X/400*, **20**(11).

Bruner, J.S. (1960); '*The process of education*'; Cambridge, Mass: Harvard University Press.

Bruner, J. S. (1966); '*Toward a theory of instruction*'; New York: Norton.

Bush, V. (1945); 'As we may think', *Atlantic Monthly* July.

Campbell, B. and Goodman, J. (1988); 'HAM: A General purpose hypertext abstract machine'; *Communication of the ACM*, **31**(7).

Carr, L.A. (1994); '*Structure and hypertext*'; Unpublished PhD, Faculty of Engineering and Applied Science, Department of Electronics and Computer Science University of Southampton.

Carroll, J.M., Mack, R.L., and Kellogg, W.A. (1988); 'Interface metaphors and user interface design'; In Helander, M. (ed.) *Handbook of Human Computer Interaction*, Amsterdam: North Holland.

Carroll, J.M. (1993); 'The Wittgenstein machine: Hypermedia for learning'; *American Journal of Psychology*, **106**(4).

Chomsky, N. (1959); 'Review of verbal behaviour'; *Language*, **35**.

Chignell, M. and Lacy, R. (1988); 'Integrating research and instruction: Project Jefferson'; *Academic Computing*, **3**(2).

Card, S.K. (1993); '*Human computer interaction*'; Hemel Hempstead: Prentice Hall Publishers.

Clark, D. (1992); 'Multimeeeja.. who needsya'; *CTISS File*, **14**(October).

Coad, P. and Yourden, E. (1990); 'Object-Oriented analysis'; *Englewood cliffs and Yourdon press*; Prentice Hall 1990.

Cohen, D. (1987); '*Oxford companion to the mind*'; New York: Oxford University Press.

Conklin, E.J. (1987); 'Hypertext: An introduction and survey'; *IEEE Computer*, **2**(9).

Conklin, E.J. and Begeman J. (1988); 'A Hypertext tool for exploratory policy discussion'; *ACM Transactions Office Information Systems*, **6**(4).

Cox, B. (1994); '*Practical pointers for university teachers*'; London: Kogan Page.

Dastbaz, M. and Kalafatis, S.P. (1993); 'Multimedia, marketing and education'; *MEG Annual Conference* July, Loughborough University.

Dastbaz, M. (2000); 'Hypermedia aided learning – a view point on delivering education in the new millennium'; *Proceedings of IEEE, Information Visualisation (IV2000) Conference*, July.

Dastbaz, M. and Kalafatis, S.P. (1996); 'Multimedia – Hypermedia vs. traditional modes of course delivery'; *Proceedings of MEG Annual Conference* July, University of Ulster (CD-ROM).

Dastbaz, M., Eldred, J. and Rodrigues, J. (1997); 'Supporting distance learning managers: A multimedia WWW system for learning support and communication'; *Proceedings of CTI-AFM 8th Annual Conference*, April.

Davis, M. and Crowther, D. (1995): 'The benefits of using multimedia in higher education'; *Active Learning*, **3**, pp. 3-6.

DeBra, P., Houben, G.J., and Kornatzky, Y. (1992); 'An extensible data model for hyperdocuments'; *Proceedings of the 4th ACM Conference on Hypertext*, Milan, pp. 222–231.

December, J. and Ginsburg, M. (1996); '*HTML 3.2 and CGI unleashed*'; Indianapolis: Sams.net Publishing.

Delclos, V.R. and Hartman, A. (1992); 'The impact of an interactive multimedia system on the quality of learning in educational psychology: An exploratory study'; *Journal of Research on Computing in Education*, April, pp. 83–93

DeRose, S. J. (1989); 'Expanding the notion of links'; *Proceedings of Hypertext '89*, pp. 238–249.

Deitel, H.M., Deitel, P.J and Nieto, T.R (2000); 'Internet & the World Wide Web – How to Program'; Prentice Hall Publishers.

Devlin, K. (1993); 'Situation theory and the design of interactive information systems'; In Rosenberg, D. and Hutchison, C. (eds.), *Design Issues in CSCW*, pp. 61-87, London: Springer-Verlag Publishers.

Dix, A., Finaly, A., Abowd, G. and Beale, R. (1998); '*Human computer interaction*'; Hemel Hempstead:Prentice Hall Publishers.

Doland, V.M. (1989); 'Hypermedia as an interpretative act'; *Hypermedia*, **1**(1).

Draper, S.W., Brown, M.I., Edgerton, E., Henderson, F.P., McAteer, E., Smith, E.D. and Watt, H.D. (1994): 'Observing and measuring the performance of educational technology'; *TLTP report* – University of Glasgow.

Dreyfus, S. and Dreyfus, H. (1980); 'A four stage model of the mental activities involved in directed skill acquisition'; Berkeley: University of California.

Drucker, P. (1997); ' Drucker on higher education'; Forbes, 3/10/97

Duffy, T.M. and Jonassen, D.H. (1991); 'Constructivism: New implications for instructional technology'; *Educational Technology*, May, pp. 7–12.

Ebbinghaus, H. (1913); '*Memory: A contribution to experimental psychology*'; (translated by H.A. Ruger) New York: Teachers College.

Egan, D., Remde, J.R., Gomez, L.M., Landaure, T.K., Eberhardt, J. and Lochbaum, C.C. (1989); 'Formative design-evaluation of SuperBook'; *ACM Transactions on Information Systems*, **7**.

Engelbart, D. and English, W. (1968); A research centre for augmenting human intellect; *IFIPS Proceedings*.

England, E and Finney, A.(2002); 'Managing Multimedia – Project Management for Web and Convergent Media', Addison Wesley Publishers.

Elsom-Cook, M. (2001); 'Principles of Interactive Multimedia'; McGraw Hill Publishing.

Everitt, R.S. (1992); '*The analysis of contingency tables*'; London: Chapman and Hall.

Ferretti, R.P. (1993); 'Interactive multimedia research questions: Results from the Delphi study'; *Journal of Special Education Technology*, **12**(2).

Frau, E., Midoro, V., Pedemonte, G.M. (1991); 'Do hypermedia systems really enhance learning? A case study on earthquake education'; *Education Technology*, **29**(1).

Friedman, M.E. (1981); 'The effects on achievement of using the computer as a problem solving tool'; *The Accountancy Review*, **LVI**(4).

Frisse, M. (1988); 'Searching for information in a hypertext medical handbook'; *Communication of the ACM*, **31**.

Furht, B. (1999); 'Handbook of Internet and Multimedia Systems and Applications'; Boca Raton, Florida: CRC Press/IEEE Press.

Ganger, P. (1990); 'Computer-based training works'; *Personnel Journal*, **69**(9).

Garzotto, F. Mainetti, L., Paolini, P. (1993): 'HDM – A model-based approach to hypertext application Design'; *ACM Transaction on Office Systems*, **11**(1).

Garzotto, F., Mainetti, L., Paolini, P.(1995): 'Hypermedia design analysis, and evaluation issues'; *Communication of the ACM*, **38**(8).

Gagne, R.M. (1985); '*The Conditions of learning and theory of instruction*', 4th edition; New York: CBS College Publication.

Ganger, P. (1990); 'Computer-based training works'; *Personnel Journal*, **69**(9).

Gibbins, P. (1997): 'Everything I know about CAL'; *Proceedings of CAL 1997 International Conference*, March, University of Exeter, pp. 1–6.

Goerne, C. (1992): 'Publishers offer novels and encyclopaedias in computer versions'; *Marketing News*, **26**(4), pp. 6.

Grant, C. (1991); 'Business presentations: You are in control'; *Business Marketing Digest*, **16**(4).

Grau, I. (1995); 'Cognitive psychology and its application to education'; Available online: http://129.7.160.115/INST5931/COGNTIVE.PSY.

Greenwell, M. (1988); 'Knowledge engineering for expert systems'; Ellis Horwood Ltd. Chichester, England

Groomer, S.M. (1981); An experiment in computer assisted instruction for introductory accountancy', *The Accountancy Review*, **LVI**(4).

Gronbaek, K. and Trigg, R. (1994); 'For a Dexter-based hypermedia system'; *The Communications of the ACM*, **2**(37).

Grubb, R.E and Selfridge, L. (1964); 'Computer tutoring in statistics'; *Computers and Automation* March, pp. 20–26.

Hac, A. (2000); 'Multimedia Application Support for Wireless ATM Networks', Prentice Hall Publications.

Haddon, K., Smith, C., Brattan, D. and Smith, T. (1995): 'Can Learning via multimedia benefit weaker students?'; *Active Learning*, **3**.

Halasz, F. and Schwartz, M. (1994): 'The Dexter Hypertext'; *Communications of the ACM*, **2**(37).

Hall, W and Lowe, D. (1999); 'Hypermedia and the Web – An Engineering Approach', John Wiely & Sons.

Hall, A. (1990); ' Seven myths of formal methods' *IEEE Software*, September 1990.

Halsall, F. (2001); 'Multimedia Communications – Applications, Networks, Protocols and Standards', Addison Wesley Publications.

Hammond, N. and Allinson, L. (1987); 'The Travel Metaphor as Design Principle and Training Aid for Navigating around Complex Systems'; In Diaper, D. and Winder, R. (eds.), *People and Computers III, Proceedings of HCI'87*, Cambridge: Cambridge University Press.

Hardman, L., Rossum, G. Bulterman, D. (1993): 'The Amsterdam hypermedia model: extending hypertext to support real multimedia'; *Hypermedia*, **5**(1).

Harris, M. and Cady, M. (1988); 'The dynamic process of creating hypertext literature'; *Education Technology*, **28**(11).

Hartley, J.R. (1978); 'An appraisal of computer assisted learning in UK'; *Programmed Learning and Educational Technology*, **15**(2).

Hawkridge, D. (1982); '*New information technology in education*'; London: Croom Helm.

Heath, S. and C. Young (1991); 'Reflections on CAL in the USA'; *CTISS File* March.

Heller, R.S. (1990); 'The role of hypermedia in education: a look at the research issues'; *The Journal of Research on Computing in Education* Summer.

Heylighen, F. (1997); 'Epistemological constructivism'; article on line, URL address: http://pespmc1.vub.ac.be/EPISTEMI.htm.

Higgins, K. and Boone, R. (1990); 'Hypertext computer study guide and the social studies achievement of students with learning disabilities, remedial students and regular education students'; *Journal of Learning Disabilities*, **23**(9), November.

Hooper, R. and Toye, I. (1975) '*Computer assisted learning in the UK*' – Report for the CTI.

Huhn, M (1992); 'Synergy: Strike 2'; *Brandweek*, **33**(37).

Hutchings, M. (1992); 'Authoring and evaluation of hypermedia for education'; *Computers Education*, **18**(1-3).

Israel, R. (1992); 'Education for the year 2000: A whole new game; *Computing Canada*, **18**(19).

Isakowitz, T., Stohr, E., & Balasubramanian, P. (1995); 'RMM: A Methodology for Structuring Hypermedia Design'. *Communications of the ACM*, **38**(8).

Jackson, P. (1990); 'Introduction to Expert Systems', *2nd Edn.* Wokingham, England: Addison-Wesley.

Jacobs, G. (1992); 'An interactive learning revolution?'; *The CTISS File*, **14**(October).

Jacobs, G. (1992); 'Hypermedia and discovery – based learning: a historical perspective'; *The British Journal of Educational Technology*, **23**(2).

James, P.N. (1992); 'Richard L. Nolan: On the importance of continuous education'; *Information Systems Management*, **9**(2).

Jamison *et al.* (1974); 'The effectiveness of alternative instructional media: a survey'; *Review of Educational Research*, **44**(1).

Jones, B. (1992); 'Multimedia with IBM'; *Journal of Management Services*, **36**(3).

Johnson, P. (1992); 'Human computer interaction', Maidenhead, Berks: McGraw-Hill Book Company.

Jonassen, D. H. (1988); 'Designing structured hypertext and structuring access to hypertext', *Educational Technology*, **28**(11).

Kafai, Y. and Resnick, M. (1996); 'Perspectives in Constructionism'; In Kafai, Y. and Resnick, M. (eds.), *'Constructionism in Practice'*, Mahwah, New Jersey: Lawrence Erlbaum Associates, Publishers.

Katona, G. (1940); *'Organising and Memorising'*; New York: Colombia University Press.

Kay, A. (1990); 'User Interface: A personal View'; In Laurel, B. (eds.), *'The art of human – computer interface design'*; Reading, Mass: Addison Wesley.

Kearsley, G. (1988); 'Authoring considerations for hypertext'; *Educational Technology* November, pp. 21–24.

Kendall, R. (1996); 'Hypertext dynamics in a life set for two', *Proceedings of the ACM Seventh Conference on Hypertext*, Washington.

Kemmis, S., Atkin, R. and Wright, E. (1977): *'How do students learn'*; Centre for applied research in education; UEA Norwich.

Keys, J. (1990); 'Stimulating students: Technology delivered instruction can spice up training sessions'; *Computer World*, **24**(43).

Keyes, J. (1990); 'Multimedia offers managers multiple business solutions'; *Computer World*, **24**(39).

Kirakowski, J. and Corbett, M. (1990); *'Effective methodology for the study of HCI'* Amsterdam: North Holland.

Knapper, C.K. (1980); *'Evaluating instructional technology'*; New York: J. Wiley and Sons.

Knussen, C., Tanner, G.R. and Kibby, M.R. (1991): 'An approach to the evaluation of hyper-media'; *Computers in Education*, **17**(1).

Kohler, W. (1927); *'The mentality of apes'*; New York: Harcourt Publishers.

Kolb, D.A. (1971); 'Individual learning styles and the learning process'; Working paper 535-71, *Sloan School of Management*, Cambridge, Mass: MIT Press.

Kolb, D.A. (1997); 'Scholarly hypertext: Self-represented complexity', *Proceedings of the Eighth ACM Conference on Hypertext*, University of Southampton.

Lamons, B. (1993); 'Look out! Here comes computer based marketing'; *Marketing News*, **27**(2).

Landow, G.P. (1989); 'Hypertext in literary education, criticism and scholarship'; *Computing Humanities*, **23.**

Landow, G.P. (1997); 'Hypertext.'; In Kelly, M. (ed.), *Encyclopaedia of Aesthetics* Oxford: Oxford University Press.

Lawton, D. (1980); *'The politics of curriculum evaluation; Curriculum education today trends and strategies'* (Edited by Tawny, D.), Schools Council Research Studies, London: Macmillan.

Lee, G. (1994); *'Object Oriented GUI Application Development'*; Hemel Hempstead: Prentice Hall Publishers.

Letza, S.R. (1991); 'The use of CAL as pre-course reading: The Bradford experience'; *Proceedings of Conference on integrating learning technology into the curriculum*, CTI publications.

Lewis, R. (1990); 'Computers in higher education teaching and learning – some aspects of research and development'; *Proceedings from the Symposium – Computers in Higher Education Teaching and Learning*; CTISS Publication June.

Lewis, C. and Rieman, J. (1993); *'Task-centred user interface design'*; Colorado University (shareware book).

Licklider, J.C.R. (1960); 'Man-computer symbiosis'; *IRE Transactions on Human Factors in Electronics* HFE-**1**(1).

Liebman, H. (1992); 'The microchip is the message'; *Mediaweek*, **2**(41).

Linn, C.M. (1992); 'How can hypermedia tools help teach programming'; *Learning and Instructions*, **2.**

Lisewski, B. and Settle, C. (1995); ' Teaching with multimedia: a case study in Weed Biology', *Active Learning* CTISS Publications, **3**(December).

Lunin, L. (1991); 'Digital or analogue: Which or both'; *Information Today*, **8**(9).

Loudon, D. and Della Bitta, A.J (1988); '*Consumer behaviour: concepts and applications*'; Maidenhead, Berks: McGraw-Hill.

Lunin, L. (1992); 'High-tech information lab opens at Library of Congress'; *Information Today*, **9**(5).

Lynch, J.P. (1994); 'Visual design for the user interface'; *Journal of Bio-Communications*, **21**(1).

MacDonald, V. (1976) '*Evaluation and control of education*', Curriculum Education Today (Ed. Tawney, D.), Reading, Mass: Macmillan.

Machan, T.R. (1974); '*The pseudo-science of B.F. Skinner*'; New Rochelle, New York: Arlington House.

McAteer, E. (1995); 'De Tudo um Pouco – A little bit of everything'; *Active Learning* CTISS Publications, **3**(December), pp. 10–15.

McCarthy, R. (1989); 'Multimedia: What the excitement's all about'; *Electronic Learning* June.

McEachern, C. (1995); 'Teaching opinion making with Authorware Professional'; Active Learning CTISS Publications, **3**(December).

McGloughlin, S.(2001); 'Multimedia Concepts and Practice'; Pearson Education.

McKeown, J.C. (1976); 'Computer assisted instructions for elementary accounting', *The Accounting Review* January.

McKenzie, J. (1977); 'Computers in the teaching of undergraduate science'; *British Journal of Educational Technology*, **8**(3).

Maguire, M.C. (1989); 'A review of human factors guidelines and techniques for the design of graphical human – computer interfaces'; In, Preece, J. and Keller, L. (eds), '*Human Computer Interaction*', Hemel Hempstead: Prentice Hall.

Marchionini, G. (1988); 'Hypermedia and learning: Freedom and chaos'; *Educational Technology* November.

Marchionini, G. and Crane, G. (1994); 'Evaluating hypermedia and learning: The Perseus project'; *ACM Transactions on Information Systems*, **12**(1).

Marshall, I.M., Samson, W.B., Dugard, P.I. and Castell, A. (1995); 'A rigorous framework for measuring development productivity and estimating the effort of multimedia courseware'; *The Proceedings of the World Conference on Computers in Education*; Edited by Tinsley, D. and Weert, T, London: Chapman and Hall.

Marshak, D. (1992); 'The multimedia malaise'; *Canadian Datasystems*, **24**(7).

Medin, D. (1976); 'Theories of discrimination learning and learning set'; In Estes, W.K. (ed.), '*Handbook of Learning and Cognitive Processes*', Volume 3, New York: Lawrence Erlbaum Associates.

Mestre, J.P. (1994); 'Cognitive aspects of learning and teaching science'; In Fitzsimmons, D. and Kerlelman, G.R. (eds.) *Teachers Enhancement for Elementary and Secondary Science and Mathemeatics: Status, Issues and Problems*, Washington, D.C: National Science Founation.

Mill, J. (1869); '*Analysis of the phenomena of the of the human mind*'; (Ed. By Bain, A., Findlater, A. and Grote, G.) Longman Publishers.

Miller, N.E. (1959); 'Liberalisation of S-R concepts. Extensions to conflict behaviour, Motivation and Social Learning. In Koch, S. (ed.), *Psychology: A Study of Science*, Vol. 2, New York: McGraw-Hill.

Miller, R.B. (1971); 'Human ease of use criteria and their trade-offs'; *IBM Report TR00.2185*, 12th April, New York: IBM Corporation.

Miller, P. (1993); 'The multimedia encyclopaedia of mammalian biology'; *The CTISS File*, **15**(April).

Mohageg, M.F. (1992); 'The influence of hypertext linking structures on the efficiency of information retrieval'; *Human Factors*, **34**(30).

Morris, S.K. (1991); 'DVI MM applications and products'; *CD-ROM Professional*, **4**(6).

Mowen, J.C. (1993); '*Consumer behaviour*'; 3rd edition, London: Macmillan Publishers.

Musthaler, L. (1993); This is not a toy; *Computerworld*, **27**(4).

Nelson, T.H. (1967); 'Getting it out of our system'; In Schechter, G. (ed.), '*Information Retrieval: A Critical Review*', Washington, DC: Thompson Books.

Nelson, T.H (1989); 'Hyperwelcom'; *Hypermedia*, **1**(1).

Nielsen, J. (1991); 'Usability considerations in introducing hypertext'; In Brown, H. (ed), '*Hypermedia/Hypertext*', London: Chapman and Hall.

Nielsen, J. (1993); '*Usability Engineering*'; Morristown, New Jersey: Academic Press.

Nielsen, J. (1995); 'Human computer interaction – Interact '95'; *Proceedings of the Interact '95 conference*, Edited by Nordby, K.; London: Chapman and Hall.

Nielsen, J. (1995); '*Multimedia and hypertext: The internet and beyond*'; New York: Harcourt Brace.

Nielsen, J (2000); 'Designing Web Usability'; New Riders Publishing.

Norman, D.A. (1988); '*The psychology of everyday things*'; New York: Basic Books Publishers.

Norman, D.A. (1993); '*Things that make us smart: Defending human attributes in the age of machine*'; Reading, Mass: Addison Wesley Publishers.

Newble, D. and Cannon, R. (1991); '*A handbook for teachers in universities and colleges*', London: Kogan Press.

O'Shea, T. and Self, J. (1983); '*Learning and Teaching with Computers*'; London: Harvester Press UK.

Ott, R.L., Mann, M.H. and Moores, C.T. (1990); 'An empirical investigation into interactive effects of students personality traits and method of instruction on student performance', *Journal of Accounting Education*, **8**.

Palmarozza, P. (1990) 'Computer based management training, a coming of age'; *Educational and Training Technology International*, **27**(2).

Papert, S. (1990); 'A Critique of Technocentrisim in thinking about the school of the future'; *E and L Memo No. 2 MIT Media Laboratory*.

Papert, S. (1996); 'Perspectives in constructionism'; In Kafai, Y. and Resnick, M. (eds.) '*Constructionism in Practice*', Mahwah, New Jersey: Lawrence Erlbaum Associates, Publishers.

Parlett, M.R. and Hamilton, D.F. (1972): 'Evaluation as illumination: A new approach to the study of innovatory programmes'; University of Edinburgh Centre for Research in Education Science, *Occasional paper No. 9*.

Parke, J.A. and Orr, A. (1992); 'New dimensions in direct marketing; catalogues find customers in the sky; new breed of infomercial generated leads'; *Target Marketing*, **15**(6).

Pask, G. (1958); '*Electronic keyboard teaching machines*', Journal of National Association of Education and Commerce, July 1958.

Pavlov, I.P. (1927); 'Conditioned reflexes' (translated by G.V. Anrep) – New York: Oxford Publishers.

Percival, F. and Ellington, J. (1988); '*A handbook of educational technology*'; London: Kogan Page Publishers.

Phillipo, J. (1989); 'Videodisc technology and HyperCard: A combination that can't be beat', *Electronic Learning*, **8**(March).

Piaget, J. (1970); '*The science of education and the psychology of the child*'; New York: Grossman Publishers.

Preece, J. (1993); 'A guide to usability, human factors in computing'; Reading, Mass: Addison – Wesley Publishing.

Pressman, R.S. (1997); 'Software Engineering: A practitioner's approach' McGraw Hill publishers.

Price R.V. (1991); '*Computer aided instruction: A guide for authors*'; California:Brooks/Cole Pacific Grove California Publications.

Quatrani, T (1998); 'Visual Modeling with Rational Rose and UML'; *Addison Wesley Longman*, Reading, MA, 1998.

Ramsden (1992); quoted in '*Rethinking university teaching*', D.Laurillard, London:Rutledge Publications

Recker, M. (1994); 'A methodology for analysing students' interaction within educational hypertext'; *Proceedings of ED-MEDIA 1994*, Vancouver, B.C. Canada, June.

Rifkin, G. (1991); 'End-user training: Needs improvement'; *Computerworld*, **25**(15).

Rines, S. (1991); 'Marketing services: The MM message'; *Marketing (UK)* April.

Ritchie, I. (1992); 'MM vs. Reality'; *The CTISS File*, **12**(October).

Rockart, J.F. and Morton, M.S. (1975); '*Computers and the learning process in higher education*'; New York: McGraw-Hill.

Romiszowski, A.R. (1993); 'Developing interactive multimedia courseware and networks – Some current issues', In Latchman, C., Willamson, J. and Henderson, L. (eds.), '*Interactive multimedia*', London: Kogan Press.

Rowland, G. (1993); 'Designing and Instructional Design'; *Educational Technology Research and Development*, **41**(1).

Rumbaugh, J. Blaha, M., Premerlani, W. Eddy, F., Lorensen, W. (1991); 'Object oriented modelling and design' *Englewood Cliffs, NJ*: Prentice Hall International.

Rumelhart, D.E. and Norman, D.A (1986); 'Representation in memory'; In Atkinson, K. and Lindsey, M. (eds.), '*Handbook of Experimental Psychology*', Chichester: Wiely and Sons Publishers.

Sangster, A. (1995); 'WWW – what can it do for education'; *Active Learning*, **2**(July).

Schwabe, D. and Rossi, G. (1995); 'The object oriented hypermedia design model'; *Communications of the ACM*, **38**(8).

Sekaran, U. (1992); '*Research methods for business: A skill building approach*'; Chichester: John Wiley and Sons Publishers.

Shackel, B. (1990); 'Human factors and usability'; In J. Preece and L. Keller (eds.), '*Human Computer Interaction*', Hemel Hempstead: Prentice Hall.

Sheth, J., & Sisodia, R. (1999); 'Revisiting Marketing's Law like Generalisations'; *Journal of the Academy of Marketing Science*, **27**(1), 1999.

Shneiderman, B (1998); 'Designing the User Interface- Strategies for Effective Human Computer Interaction'; Addison Wesley Publications.

Shneiderman, B., Brethauer, D., Plaisant, C. and Potter, R. (1989); 'The HyperTIES electronic encyclopaedia: An evaluation based on three museum installation'; *Journal of American Sociology Information Science*, **40**(3).

Shulman, R.E. (1992); 'MM . . . A high-tech solution to industry's training malaise'; *Supermarket Business*, **47**(4).

Siegel, D. (1997); 'Creating Killer Web Sites'; Hayden Bokks.

Skinner, B.F. (1938); *The behaviour of organisms*', New York: Alperton Publishers.

Skinner, B.F. (1968); *The technology of teaching meredith*', New York: Alperton Publishers.

Sloane, A. (1996); 'Multimedia Communication', McGraw Hill Publishing.

Smith, J.B. and Weiss, S.F. (1988); 'Hypertext'; *The Communications of the ACM*, **31**(7).

Smith, R.B. (1992); 'Computer-based training is designed for interactive learning experience', *Occupational Health and Safety*, **61**(12).

Spears, E. (1987); 'Innovative visual techniques create powerful images of lifestyle'; *Sales and Marketing Management in Canada*, **28**(2).

Spence, K. W. (1956): *Behaviour theory and conditioning*'; Yale University: New Haven Publishers.

Stanton, N. (1991); 'Hypermedia considerations, concerns and conclusions'; *Proceedings of a Conference on the Integration of Computer Based Teaching Materials in Higher Education*'. Bradford Management Centre, CTISS.

Stapleton, J. (1998); 'A quality approach to to rapid application development' SQM issue 25, 1998.

Stotts, P. D. and Furuta, R. (1989); 'Petri-net-based hypertext: Document structure with browsing semantics'; *ACM Transactions on Information Systems*, **7**(1).

Smyth, M., Anderson, B., Knott, R. and Alty, L. (1995); 'Reflections on the design of the interface metaphors'; In Nordby, K. (ed.), *Human Computer Interaction – Interact '95*', pp. 339–345, London: Chapman and Hall Publishers.

Tannenbaum, R.S. (1998); 'Theoretical Foundations of Multimedia'; Computer Science Press.

Thorndike, E. L. (1898): 'Animal Intelligence: An Experimental Study of the Associative Processes in Animals'; *Psychological Review Monograph Supplements*, **2**(4) (whole No. 8).

Thorpe, M. (1988); *Evaluating open and distance learning*'; Essex: Longman.

Tsai, S.Y.W. and Pohl, N.F. (1978); 'Students achievement in computer programming: lectures vs. Computer aided instruction'; *Journal of Experimental Education*, **46**(2).

Tull, D.S. and Hawkins, D.I. (1993); *Marketing research: Measurement and method*'; New York: Macmillan Publishing.

Turkel, S. (1984); *The second self: Computers and the human sprit*'; New York: Simon and Schuster.

Vaughan, T. (1998); 'Multimedia Making It Work'; Osborne Publishing.

Vaughan, T. (1994); 'Multimedia Making It Work'; Osborne Publishing

Van Dam, A. (1987); 'Hypertext '87 – Keynote Address'; *Communication of the ACM*, **31**(7), pp. 887–895.

Vandergrift, K.E. (1988); 'Hypermedia: breaking the tyranny of the text ', *School Library Journal*, **35**(November).

Viau, R. and Larivee (1993); 'Learning tools with hypertext: An experiment'; *Computers Education*, **20**(1).

Vitiello, J. (1990); 'Worker education: A magic act'; *Computerworld*, **24**(52, 53).

Voss, B. (1992); 'A presentation update'; *Sales and Marketing Management*, **144**(14).

Vygotsky, L. (1962); *Thought and language*', Cambridge, MA.: MIT Press.

Vygotsky, L. (1978); *Mind in society*', Cambridge, MA: Harvard University Press.

Ulrich, K. (1999); 'Flash for Windows and Macintosh', Peachpit Press.

Watson, B. (1948); *Behavior*', New York, MIT Press.

White, D. (1989); 'The banking information service: Spreading the message'; *Banking World* (UK), **7**(10).

Wells, J.B., Layne, B.H. and Allen, D. (1991); 'Management development training and learning styles'; *Public Productivity and Management Review*, **14**(4).

Wertherimer, M. (1959); '*Productive thinking*'; New York: Harper and Row Publishers.

Whalley, P. (1990); 'Models of hypertext structure and learning'; In Jonassen, D. H. and Mandi, H. (eds.) '*Designing hypermedia for learning*', New York: Springer-Verlag.

Wilson, B., Teslow, J. and Osman-Jouchoux, R. (1995); 'The impact of Constructivism and post-modernism on instructional design fundamentals'; In Seels, B.B. (ed.), '*Instructional design fundamentals: A review and reconsideration*', Englewood Cliffs NJ: Educational Technology Publications.

Wilson, B.G. (1997); 'The Post-modern Paradigm'; In Dills, C. and Romiszowski, A.R. (eds.), '*Instructional design: The state of the art*', Vol.3, Englewood Cliffs NJ: Educational Technology Publications.

# Index